The Joy of Jumping

THE
JOY OF
JUMPING

A Complete Jump-Rope Program for Health, Looks, and Fun

---

by Greg Campbell

Richard Marek Publishers, New York

796.2

9-79   B+J   895

Library of Congress
78-18011

Cloth, ISBN: 0-399-90015-2
Paper, ISBN: 0-399-90010-1

Printed in the United States of America

Acknowledgments

This is the place where someone who is still a stranger to you plugs people who have been friends to him in the preparation of a manuscript. Some people have contributed greatly to this work in a variety of ways. Notably:

My wife Janelle has been more than an inspiration. She has been a partner in fitness. We jump together.

Dr. Jack Baker's expertise in the physiological benefits of cardiovascular exercise and the role rope skipping plays in attaining fitness has been of tremendous value to me.

I would also like to thank Muhammad Ali, who has been my greatest inspiration for the past fourteen years. (Ever since the Liston knockout, February 25, 1964.) Without Ali, many of us might have gone through life not knowing we too could be the "greatest" in what we do.

Frank Prentup and Joyce Engelson have been essential in the development of this book. Frank, for developing many of today's most popular rope-jumping steps. Joyce, as my stony-eyed editor, has kept this book to the point.

And special thanks to Carl Ames, whose research and help in writing has actually made this book possible. He's also jumping rope now.

And special thanks also to Bruce Hoag for his photographs, and to Michael Hahn for his illustrations.

And special recognition to you for taking a crack at my program.

Thanks, gang.

Dedicated to my mother, June Catherine
Campbell, whose encouragement and guidance
in my career and in sports and whose motivation
to high ideals of personal accomplishment and
achievement have inspired me throughout my life.

CONTENTS

Fitness does not have to be achieved at the cost
  of bodily discomfort
Working up a sweat is not essential to fitness
You do not need to wear a sweat suit or a rubberized suit
  to stay warm while exercising
You do not need to keep warm after exercising
You do not need a cold shower after exercise
Consuming additional protein will not give you more energy
Eating sugar will not give you the right kind of energy burst
You do not need to take salt tablets while exercising
You do not need to abstain from drinking while exercising
You do not need more sleep while in an exercise program
You do not need to exercise an hour every day
You do not have to suffer to become fit

Cardiovascular fitness must be achieved gradually by means
of a week-by-week program of increasing difficulty

It's efficient. It's effective.
It's inexpensive
It's convenient
It's not boring
It's practical
It's simple
It's fun

The Joy of Jumping

I.
Hop To It

I think I'm a fanatic.

I fantasize that the entire country is jumping rope. Office workers, housewives, dentists, disc jockeys, firemen, pre-schoolers, retired carpenters, post-cardiac patients, everybody jumping rope every day. Alone and together. At family get-togethers, picnics, factory rest periods, office breaks, on sidewalks, porches, roofs, living rooms, at the motorcycle club houses, and in the Oval Office.

It is happening now. It's not all a dream of mine. Football teams, college and professional, are jumping. Junior high school gym classes are jumping. Jumping rope is the fastest growing fitness exercise in America. Its popularity is only beginning. And, pages from now, you are going to find out why.

Seven years ago, I wasn't a fanatic. I was a "closet" jumper. When I first started jumping rope, I'd hide. A professional hockey player and coach jumping rope? C'mon. That's only for boxers and little girls singing, "I love coffee, I love tea . . ."

Forgive a professional athlete for saying so but, to me, most exercise is boring. Do you agree? It's time-consuming. It's hard work. And if it's boring to me, I can imagine how tedious and painful it must be to you.

Although I still made part of my living from team sports, I noticed I just wasn't exercising the way I should. I had begun losing that discipline and drive I used to have.

Worse yet, I found myself with less time and even less desire to devote to the rigorous physical fitness routines I had learned from high school and college coaches.

Was my "gung ho" gone? I knew I still needed to work out, to keep fit, not only for my health. My livelihood depended on it. But the spirit of 100 percent devotion I used to give to the old programs was gone.

Suddenly, there were so many new things in my life. I was just too busy and no longer had the time to give. The ancient exercise programs demanded too much of my time. I had no time now. And I no longer had

1

the faith in my old exercise routines. I had to find a new way of keeping fit. A modern way.

I tried a lot of exercise routines which took time, money, space—or worse, all three. I also found a new psychological barrier. I found myself rejecting any program which brought back memories of "old school" calisthenics. I even resented jogging because it reminded me of the laps I had to take after practice every day while in school.

To tell you the truth, I was looking for a shortcut to staying in shape. I found it. The jump rope.

Since that time seven years ago when I first started jumping in private, I've made dozens of appearances with my jump-rope act in public, and on television programs across the country.

I hold one of the world records in rope jumping and have designed my own jump-rope program, which I want to share with you.

Wait a minute. Put the book down and make an appointment with your doctor for a checkup. Right now. Closed? Tomorrow morning, then. First thing. Nothing is more important in a fitness program than a professional, medical analysis of your present level of fitness. This issue is so important I'm going to nag you about it in every chapter.

Now, I'd like to tell you what I've learned about exercise. I'm a fanatic, all right. I have extremist views which challenge the mythological concept that to get fit, you must suffer. The idea that you must grunt and groan, sweat and bleed, gasp and ache to feel better is as unfounded as the tale that toads cause warts. The "it's got to hurt to be good" philosophy of fitness has been perpetrated upon us by gym instructors, coaches and health spas all these years, and we bought it. Now we can forget it. You can become fit in minutes a day without pain, boredom or expense.

That sounds too easy, doesn't it? My jump-rope program is work. It's not hard labor, but it is work. It is effort. You cannot become fit without any work. But I think you are going to love this job of rope skipping. You are going to love getting fit.

Being fit means being younger, stronger, shapelier, and happier.

Listen, I've never felt better in my life. I sleep better, get up easier, and feel less tension. I live life to the fullest. To me, there's a bounce in my step as I anticipate life's challenges with a power of energy that can come only from knowing I am the best I can possibly be: I am in shape. I am fit. And I haven't worked all that hard to get there. I haven't spent anything like the boring, groaning effort I expended in my professional hockey workout days.

But I haven't missed a day jumping rope. It's that simple.

II.
The Exercise Myths

(And the Greg Campbell Myth-Breakers)

Somewhere along the line, exercise got a bad name: masochism. You know, the old "it only does you good when it hurts" idea? No wonder you've been putting off beginning an exercise program for yourself. You've been led to believe that to get fit, you must suffer.

Some people actually become masochistic about their health: they come to enjoy suffering.

If you aren't as stiff as a board the day after you start exercising, you can be sure it is doing you no good at all, right? And the only sure way to get rid of all that stiffness is to exercise more the next day until you feel you can go no further, and then do a little more?

So you plan to exercise, and then you think about all that suffering, and that you must put some time aside to suffer tomorrow. And tomorrow comes and you think, "Well, I've had a rough day. I'll start suffering (exercising) tomorrow." You already have begun suffering in another way: guilt. And guilt can equal stress. You feel guilty about putting off getting the exercise you need. Guilt doesn't aid health.

The very thought of acquiring a habit of sweating and straining, struggling to go a little further than you think you can, until those little spots start appearing before your eyes, is enough to frighten away all but the most zealous and foolhardy fitness nuts.

Maybe you were trapped by the myths about exercise in a school gym class years ago.

Well, that was years ago. Times and attitudes have changed. And it's time some of these myths were destroyed, once and for all. I want you to look forward to my program in anticipation of *having a good time* while getting in shape.

One statement regarding fitness has survived, however, and remains sound. Before any fitness program is begun, you must have your physical condition assessed by your physician. Checkups are essential regardless of what you plan to do about your state of fitness.

Walking into your doctor's office for a physical should be your first exercise.

Okay, let's get the myths out of the way now. When the dust has settled, you will discover that becoming fit is so easy, so simple, it's almost laughable. What follows are my Greg Campbell myth-breakers.

Not long ago, I drove past a woman who was putting in that extra effort while jogging. Even from my car, I could tell she was sweating and straining for just one more block. Her eyes were bulging and her tongue was hanging out as she struggled for just one step more than yesterday. It was all I could do to keep from stopping the car and saying to her: "You don't have to do this to get fit! Somebody told you you have to, but you don't. It's not a matter of how *much*, but how *little* exercise you need to keep fit!"

FITNESS DOES NOT HAVE TO BE ACHIEVED AT THE COST OF BODILY DISCOMFORT

You should never suffer from stiffness or exhaustion. Instead, you should start with a series of gentle exercises in a balanced program designed to slowly improve the condition of your body. Exercises that are vigorous and too strenuous can hurt you. Of course, you will huff and puff during my program, as you will in any worthwhile fitness plan. But any strain or pain you feel as the result of exercise means you are either in the wrong fitness program or at the wrong point in the right fitness program.

WORKING UP A SWEAT IS NOT ESSENTIAL TO FITNESS

As a matter of fact, working up a sweat could be downright unhealthy. Here's why. As you get hotter, more blood moves out toward your skin. Notice how you get red-faced during strenuous exercise? When your blood moves to your skin, it deprives your muscles of the volume of blood they need to function effectively.

During exercise, they body's heat production is increased. That heat is dissipated through the blood being brought to the surface of your skin, which allows radiation of the heat. If additional cooling is needed, the sweat glands begin to secrete water and the body is further cooled by evaporation of perspiration.

If you think you are losing weight by sweating, you're wrong. You are only losing water temporarily. Sweating does not "clean the pores" either. There doesn't seem to be any evidence that sweating is of any value in removing toxic materials from the body. Sweating exercises your cooling system. That's all. Fitness is developed by exercising the muscles of the body, not the sweat glands!

YOU DO NOT NEED TO WEAR A SWEAT SUIT OR A RUBBERIZED SUIT TO STAY WARM WHILE EXERCISING

You are better off in as little clothing as possible, to stay cool. Again, excessive sweating is not necessarily an indication that you've had a good workout. And the more clothing you wear, the harder your body has to work to cool off, particularly if you wear specially treated clothing (such as rubberized or plastic lined or coated, or even just synthetics) which does not permit body heat to escape.

YOU DO NOT NEED TO KEEP WARM AFTER EXERCISING

Somebody got the idea that you could catch cold more easily after exercise and decided maybe putting on more clothes after the workout would protect you.

Wrong. You are better off leaving your sweater off until you cool off.

Remember this one? This is a doozy: "After your workout, take a hot shower followed by a cold one." Can you follow the reasoning of that? I can't. Neither can physiologists.

YOU DO NOT NEED A COLD SHOWER AFTER EXERCISE

All a cold shower or bath will do for you is save a little on your next heating bill. Jumping into cold water suddenly can constrict the blood vessels of the heart and aggravate problems such as angina.

Do what you normally would do. If you need a bath or shower or want one, take it. If it feels good, do it.

But if you bathe because you have perspired heavily from working out or you need to feel warm water soothing aching and tired muscles, you are in the wrong fitness program. If you are in my jump-rope program, odds are you won't even work up a sweat.

Here's another myth: "For extra energy, eat plenty of protein to sustain an exercise program." Wrong again.

CONSUMING ADDITIONAL PROTEIN WILL NOT GIVE YOU MORE ENERGY

Athletes who eat steak at every meal to build themselves up are, in fact, not doing anything of the kind. Protein is acquired from almost any food, and in any reasonable diet you automatically get enough, even more than you really need.

Protein cannot be stored up in the body as a source of energy. Your body will, however, yield protein as a fuel source as a last resort. And even then, protein can provide only about 5 percent of your total fuel capacity at best.

The value of proteins are in the building of new tissues, enzymes and hormones. Proteins are essential because they offer amino acids that cannot be manufactured in the body.

So when your body calls upon its protein as a source of energy, it does so at the expense of your body structures. Fats and carbohydrates are used first. If protein is being used, you are wasting your body. Proteins, therefore, cannot and should not be considered a quick calorie or energy source.

EATING SUGAR WILL NOT GIVE YOU THE RIGHT KIND OF ENERGY BURST

Glucose, or sugar as we know it, provides energy, all right, but not significantly or even, many authorities believe, properly. It provides empty calories. (Sugar or glucose taken in quantity before exercise could even stimulate an unwanted insulin reaction.)

Later on, we'll talk more about exercise and diet. For the moment, bear in mind that an important aspect of fitness is the measure of fat in your body. Your weight may not have changed over the years, but you find yourself getting flabby. Your weight has not changed but the percentage of fat in your body has!

Taking extra sugar for "instant fuel" means your body does not have to burn its fat. The fat just lays there, untouched.

If you engage in strenuous exercise longer than an hour, however, it is necessary to replace lost body sugar. Do so sensibly and moderately, balancing your carbohydrate intake with other nutritional elements.

Besides, you're not running in the Boston Marathon tomorrow or planning to break my world record in jumping this evening. You don't need any cheap extra energy trick.

Oh, remember the salt tablets? I suppose the recommendation to take those in fitness programs had to do with the loss of salt during exercise through sweating. Sorry. Extra salt can do more harm than good.

6

You do not need to take salt tablets while exercising

First of all, because you are engaged in the perfect exercise, your perspiration will be minimal and so will your salt loss. Should you find yourself in strenuous activity on a hot day, however, keep this in mind. The salt you do lose should be replaced. But you don't lose much. So use salt as you normally do, with food, and *after* you exercise. If you do it this way, you will adjust the balance easily.

Salt tablets taken before exercise can dry out your body cells and cause nausea and muscular cramp. When, and if you do take them, make sure it's not on an empty stomach and it is with plenty of water.

The next myth that I absolutely must debunk before you come along with me on your journey to fitness with ease is this: "No matter how thirsty you are, never drink while you're exercising." More deprivation through exercise!

Listen, if you're thirsty, drink. Especially while you are exercising. (Stop jumping first, though. You're not ready for the trick stuff yet!)

You do not need to abstain from drinking while exercising

There is no foundation to the old idea that drinking during exercise leads to cramps. If you don't replace the fluid lost through physical activity, the body dehydrates and additional strain is placed on the heart. Don't drink if you don't feel thirsty, but do drink if you do. It's that simple.

It makes sense that drinking a lot of fluids immediately before exercising might give you an undesirable feeling of fullness and the sound of Grandma's old wringer washer as you jump.

Whatever you drink, make certain it is not alcohol. Alcohol constricts the arteries leading to the heart. A combination of this state and vigorous activity can be very dangerous. If you've consumed an alcoholic beverage, wait at least two hours before exercising.

Our next myth has to do with sleep: "Get more sleep. And make sure you catch up on your sleep. If you only get six hours one night, sleep ten hours the next night."

You do not need more sleep while in an exercise program

First of all, you cannot store up sleep. Sleeping six hours one night and ten the next to maintain a two-day average of eight hours is a nice plan on paper, but the body just doesn't work that way. Ever had a rough week and said to yourself: "Tomorrow is Saturday. I'm going to sleep late and charge up."

So what happens? You sleep until noon and wake up hoping to feel full of energy again. Instead, you feel weak, fuzzy and lazy all day. And you say to yourself, "Boy, I must have gotten too much sleep." That's exactly what happened. For us grown-ups, sleeping past about nine hours can actually deprive you of energy no matter how much you may have missed the day or week before.

During your first six hours of sleep, your body recharges. After about eight or nine hours, however, the charge starts to slip. The body begins to run down. Your heartbeat slows, circulation starts to lag, and you take in less oxygen. You wake up weaker than you would have been had you risen earlier. You overslept. So just try to make sure you get those six or eight hours of sleep every night. Whatever your body requires (and there is some variety and difference in individual needs; ask your doctor), if you don't make your quota one night, remember you cannot catch up the next night.

Our final myth has to do with time: "You should exercise for at least an hour every day. Any less is a waste of time." Let's see now. If you exercise for an hour, you'll probably work up a sweat. That means a shower, maybe a rest, and a change of clothes. Two hours. I don't have two extra hours a day, do you? I'll tell you what I have got, frankly. I have ten minutes a day to exercise. And that's all you and I need. Ten minutes a day.

YOU DO NOT NEED TO EXERCISE AN HOUR EVERY DAY. FIVE TO FIFTEEN MINUTES ARE ENOUGH IF YOU ARE IN THE RIGHT PROGRAM

And right now, you're in the right program because you have this book and you have read this far. I guarantee this program.

You don't have to exercise every day either. I said earlier I haven't missed a day jumping rope. Well, I'm a fanatic. Besides, I'm a professional rope-skipper. That just occurred to me, but it is true. Although you might have your dreams, I don't think you're out to break world records or develop a nightclub act. You want to feel better and look better the fastest, easiest, happiest way there is.

So don't jump every day. *Jump five days a week.* Pamper yourself. Take a couple of days off. If you follow my program, I have no fears about your becoming sedentary during your two days off. You'll feel the urge to move as automatically as you feel your teeth getting furry. You may not jump, but I know you will move, run, stretch, play tennis, golf, or do something beyond normal exertion. You have to. It's a part of the new you. It's going to be downright natural that you do so. Exciting, isn't it? It's so easy.

So let's take one last look at our mythical masochist of exercise before we say good-bye forever. There he is over there. You can hear him grunting and groaning, sweating heavily in his rubber suit. Nearby there is a pile of salt tablets and sugar and protein supplements, but all he really wants is a forbidden long drink of water.

Right now, he's struggling for just one more strain than yesterday. He's been going at it for almost an hour now. Soon he can relax in a nice ice cold shower. Tomorrow he'll be stiff as a board, but he'll work it off. Can you imagine yourself suffering so? Me neither. So forget him. The myth has ended.

You DO NOT HAVE TO SUFFER TO BECOME FIT
In fact, I think you're going to love every minute of it.

One factual footnote to our chapter of myths. Not enough people realize how important it is to see their doctor for a checkup before plunging into any strenuous exercise, including this one. Before you jump, play tennis, jog, join a softball team, play football in the park on Sunday, see your doctor. We all need regular checkups anyway, so why not combine your physical exam with a clean bill of health for your jump-rope program?

III.
The Heart of the Matter

Now that you have cleared your mind of those frightening fallacies about fitness, I hope you are ready to give this matter of getting into shape another try. My way.

My way, as you know by now, is jumping rope. In the coming chapters, I'll show you how this simple, age-old exercise does what it does.

But first, you need to absorb some physiological savvy. Because whether you plan to exercise to lose weight, increase stamina, improve coordination, strengthen your legs, reduce stress, or even to enhance your sex life (see Chapter VII), the primary benefit of any correct exercise program is the improvement of your heart rate. In other words, exercise properly and you will strengthen your heart. Some types of exercise do this. Others do not. Rope skipping does!

Today's medical authorities agree that cardiovascular fitness is the most valid indicator of a person's relative physical fitness. If your heart, lungs, and circulatory system are in good shape, the rest of your body is usually in good shape, too.

The paradox here is: a strong heart is a slow heart. Through exercise, you are going to *slow down* your heart rate and *increase its ability to slow down sooner after exercise.* When Roger Bannister began training to break the four-minute mile, his resting heart rate was in the seventies. His resting heart rate after breaking the record was measured at about 37 beats per minute!

On the average, the resting heart rate for men is around 74 beats per minute. Women average closer to 78 beats per minute. It has yet to be understood why women have higher heart rates. The point is, the lower your resting heart rate and the more rapidly your heart reaches its resting rate after exercise, the stronger your heart and cardiovascular system is.

To understand how this whole fantastic system works—and it's important that you do—understand that your body is going through a continual energy crisis. It needs fuel to convert into energy. In our part of the world, fuel is no problem . . . unless it is the problem of too much fuel. Food is the fuel for our bodies. The energy crisis is the lack of oxy-

10

gen needed to convert that fuel into energy. Without the right oxygen supply, that fuel turns to fat and accumulates. Too much stored fuel can result in high blood pressure, poor circulation and heart problems.

While fuel can be stored, oxygen is a fleeting thing. It cannot be stored. Unless your cardiovascular system can deliver enough oxygen for proper fuel conversion, the system becomes atrophic.

Before we get more technical here, I'd like to tell you what we're really talking about so you can use it as a guide from here on. What we're really talking about is getting your body to use more oxygen. It's as simple as jumping rope. Sounds a bit greedy, but the fact remains that the more oxygen you take in, the more energy your body *and* your mind can put out.

How does it work? Your heart was designed to work. Without work to do, the heart becomes smaller, less efficient, and pumps less blood. A slower bloodstream means delivery of less oxygen and elimination of less waste. Filter systems clog and capillary canals close up, cheating tissues of needed nourishments. Your body's demand for energy will exceed its capacity to produce it.

There's an old saying that applies to your heart very accurately: Use it or lose it. *Exercise the most important muscle in your body by exercising the muscular system.* That's the way to reach that perpetual pump.

Become big-hearted. Caution: An enlarged heart is a medical problem. A large, muscular heart is a medical solution. Your stronger, muscular heart is a medical solution. Your stronger, larger heart will pump more blood from the venous system (veins) into the arterial system (arteries) with less effort, according to its *size, strength,* and *elasticity*.

Now, the condition of your heart can directly influence the condition of your lungs.

About six liters of air are contained in the lungs of the average adult male, only a fraction of which is exchanged with each breath at rest.

A strong heart helps you to expand the vital capacity of the lungs, which is the amount of air you can exhale after taking as deep a breath as possible. It is important to exchange as much air as you can. Depending on your age, you can exchange between four and five liters, bringing fresher supplies of oxygen more often and faster to your heart.

So exercise strengthens the heart in three ways. First, the heart's muscle tone is improved. Second, the vessel system is kept open and clean, maintaining maximum circulation. Finally, exercise improves the coordination of the fibers of the heart as they pump out blood.

In other words, through exercise, arteries are massaged and become more elastic. Thus the flow of blood becomes freer and easier. Capillaries spread and stretch, sending greater amounts of blood to nerve and muscle fibers. Blood pressure drops. The heart rate drops.

As you continue to prepare for jumping rope, the perfect exercise, think about your most miraculous of all muscles. Think about it getting stronger, bigger, more supple and resilient. Think about your life's pump pushing energy throughout your body in record time and volume with possibly half the effort that it's making now. (Suppose you lowered your resting heart rate from 78 to 39?)

As the pump grows stronger, the volume of your blood increases. New, lively red corpuscles by the millions form bone marrow and join the bloodstream, reviving tired blood. Fatty substances are reduced. This whole fantastic process, this new growth, is what is going to convert fatness into trimness, listlessness to liveliness, tension into relaxation, even worry into joy.

Exercising your heart may not exactly be what you had in mind. You're concerned about how your body looks, and I'm concentrating on a part of your body no one sees. Look at it this way. You are getting more than you imagined. My program will give you what you want as side benefits of a stronger heart! You can't lose.

Now, just raising the heartbeat rate without involving the muscles doesn't work. Becoming upset or alarmed increases your heartbeat but does not cause your muscles to work. But that's not exercise. Exercise occurs when your muscles squeeze blood through the body by contracting and expanding. If the heart has nothing to push against, it could be strained rather than exercised.

You need to use your muscles to strengthen your heart. Not the back-breaking, painful mythology of exercise we talked about earlier, but the simple practice of raising your heartbeat rate to between 120 and 140 beats per minute over a short, sustained period of between two and fifteen minutes.

CARDIOVASCULAR FITNESS MUST BE ACHIEVED GRADUALLY BY MEANS OF A WEEK-BY-WEEK PROGRAM OF INCREASING DIFFICULTY

Cardiologists have studied this process so carefully they are able to guide cardiac patients into rope jumping or other exercise programs in order to gradually lower the pulse rate through the expenditure of short bursts of energy. The exact level of intensity and duration of these exercises is determined by pulse rate. Physicians thus are able to gradually condition or recondition the heart through exercise by monitoring the pulse rate.

According to Dr. Kaare Rodahl in his book *Be Fit For Life*, recent studies indicate that exercise may even allow the development of new blood vessels in the heart muscle after an occlusion has occurred. In other words, exercise may not only protect a healthy heart, since physical activity causes many more blood vessels to develop in the muscle tissue—exercise may also help to heal a heart that is sick.

Incidentally, if you have a real or suspected heart condition, do not undertake my jumping program or any other exercise program without a doctor's advice. In fact, have a good, thorough checkup first, no matter what you believe your state of health to be.

My program is easy and simple, but it still calls for work, work beyond your normal capacity, whatever level it may be for you. Determine first your present state of fitness from an authority.

Now that you know what you're exercising and why, let's look at the perfect exercise.

IV.
The Perfect Exercise

Posing an even stronger argument about the value of exercise would be a waste of time. You feel you could use some exercise. You know you need it. It's just that there are some things in your way. Like what exercise can do the most for you in the least amount of time with the least effort and expense? Let's take a look at some of the alternatives. I've tried most of them.

First, there are the boring exercises. You know the kind. Sit-ups and knee bends, for example. Boring exercises usually must be combined in a series to create a well rounded program. Jack LaLanne and Debbie Drake helped you through the boring exercises, remember? "Up-down, up-down, faster, faster, stand up, fall down, up-down, faster. Now, this one's for the stomach. You'll really feel this one." You really felt that one, too. And exercise instructors are always a little bit faster than you and always smiling as if those calisthenics felt good and were fun. Boring exercises are often painful, too. I don't think exercise has to be boring and it should *not* be painful. Ever. So much for calisthenics. Takes too long, it's boring, it hurts, and you need a leader.

Next, there are the boring exercises that require equipment instead of TV or instructors. The equipment serves as a force to work against. There are weights that you lift and weights that you pull. Boards that incline and hold your legs down so you can do sit-ups properly. Springs, wires and tubing that you pull and stretch. Most exercise machines have two distinct disadvantages: they are expensive and they will not fit in a purse or a coat pocket.

Well, how about a trip to the gym or the spa? You could purchase a membership at the local health club. That's great. A lot of people, with the time and money, are doing that. In some areas of the country, there are lists of people waiting to join a health club when someone else runs out of time or money. Within your grasp, at a club, are dozens of exercise machines, a gym, a pool, gymnastic equipment, and the rewards of a long day of exercise: shower, sauna, masseuse and heat lamps. I found myself joining, with good intentions about going every day or, at least, a few times a week. But conflicts in scheduling kept coming up and I went less and less. I felt guilty and rationalized: Well, sure I didn't exercise the past few days, but I'll make it up at the club next week. Or next month. I got discouraged. I learned that health clubs *are* good . . . as an addition to your regular exercise program. And if you can afford one and there's a good one nearby where membership is available. If not, forget it. *Let your jump rope be your health club.*

How about sports. Tennis, for example, is a great all-around exercise. One of the few sports that rank high as such. Relying on a partner for a fitness program, however, just doesn't work. First of all, finding a regular partner for tennis or water-skiing or square dancing gets wearisome.

"How about tennis sometime?"

"Sure, when?"

"Tonight?"

"Nope, can't. How about tomorrow night?"

"No. I have a meeting. How about Wednesday?"

"Wednesday. Oops. Wife's birthday. How about Thursday?"

"Thursday? Well, I've only got an hour. Make it Friday."

"OK. Friday it is."

Friday, it rains. Play at an indoor tennis arena. Figure on four-to-ten dollars an hour plus membership and be sure you call far in advance for a court reservation.

Relying on a partner for exercise poses another disadvantage. You progress only at the rate your partner or opponent does. If the two of you are not a fairly even match, one of you gets less out of the activity. So the trouble with tennis and similar activities as your *regular daily exercise* activity has to do with finding a regular, suitable daily partner. And in many cities and towns, it also means getting a permit, finding a place to play, and booking days in advance. Tennis also costs money, not just for equipment, but for the club membership and/or the per hour cost of playing under a popular "bubble" or private court.

Sports like tennis rank high as oxygen-consuming cardiovascular exercise. Indulge in them while you are on a regular exercise program. But don't let yourself be trapped by excusing yourself from exercise because you can't assemble the necessary materials for your chosen exercise—like partners, time and money. Finding one steady, effective partner is not easy. Finding nine guys for touch football, ten girls for softball, eight women and men for volleyball is tougher than finding a partridge in a pear tree.

Speaking of sports, coeducational team sport is a great way to augment an exercise program. Coed softball, volleyball and football are all something you can count on for fun and physical activity once or twice a week. I've seen teams with an age variance of forty years keeping up with each other.

You see, I don't want to discourage your joining the team or experiencing a non-individual sport. In fact, I think you'll want to even more once you begin my program. Just don't rely on sports as your basic fitness program. It won't work.

Walking is good, and you should walk whenever and wherever possible. Walk to places you've always driven to. Take the stairs instead of the elevator. Walk whenever you have the time, weather and safety. It will add to your fitness program, but it cannot be your fitness program.

But walking as your main exercise takes too much time. Bicycling attracts dogs. A trip to the gym or spa is inconvenient and usually out of the question. Calisthenics are boring.

What about jogging? A great exercise. And if it weren't for the dogs nipping at your heels, the auto exhaust smoke and traffic, the rain and snowstorms, the bitter cold, the unpleasant jarring of the spine, step after step on concrete, the potholes and chuckholes waiting out of sight, jogging could be the perfect exercise. But it isn't.

In addition to tennis, swimming, golfing, softball, hiking, jogging, running-in-place (really boring!) . . . or, instead of all of them together, you need a regular, almost daily, short exercise that is not exhausting. An exercise you can do just about anywhere at anytime. More than that, you need an exercise *program*. One that develops along with you. One that grows in complexity, fun, skill, and challenge as you require or wish. The perfect exercise is a match between what you want and what you need. What you need is an exercise that will strengthen your heart and lungs and expand the possibility of a longer life. A life-giving exercise.

Not all types of exercise offer what you need. Isometric exercises, for example, are for people who can do little else. Isometrics are exercises in which muscular effort works against objects that cannot be moved. Ever hear of Charles Atlas? He offered to build your body and keep bruisers from kicking sand in your face in front of your best girl at the beach. Atlas introduced "dynamic tension" exercises in 1921. They were isometric in nature. Isometrics do increase strength and muscle tone rapidly. They are easy exercises and can be done anywhere.

What isometrics will *not* do is improve the heart and blood system or the lungs. They will *not* increase oxygen intake. They are not enough.

Isotonic exercises are like isometrics except there is more movement by you or the object you are straining against. Everything from pitching horseshoes, archery, tumbling, and gymnastics to weightlifting and calisthenics are classified as isotonic. They are great exercises for warming up to or in addition to aerobic exercise but, in themselves, cannot give you what you need.

Aerobic exercise. You've probably heard the word "aerobic." Dr.

16

Kenneth Cooper's book *Aerobics* supplanted *Royal Canadian Air Force Exercises* not long ago. Aerobic simply means: oxygen-consuming. That's us. Along with the cat, plants, amoebas and all living creatures on this earth. We're aerobic. Hello, fellow aerob! Here are the exercises made exclusively for us. Aerobic exercises gradually increase heart action and sustain it at an even, rhythmic pace until a new, higher level of oxygen income is demanded over a short period of time. The blood vessels are expanded, the blood flow is increased, and the body works beyond average effort. Aerobic exercises are those which commit you to consume more oxygen. Running, rowing, swimming, tennis . . . *and rope jumping are aerobic exercises.*

Jumping rope is the kind of aerobic exercise you need. It is also the kind you want. It's the perfect exercise. Here's why:

IT'S EFFICIENT. IT'S EFFECTIVE

Jumping rope is the best all-around exercise you can find. There is nothing you can spend less time on that gives you more results. Not even jogging. A 1968 Harvard Step Test administered by Dr. Jack Baker (see next chapter) divided ninety-two male students into two groups. Group I skipped rope ten minutes daily for six weeks and Group II jogged thirty minutes daily for the same period of time. The results were reported in the *American Association for Health, Physical Education and Recreation Research* quarterly and stated: "A ten minute daily program of rope skipping is as efficient as a 30-minute daily program of jogging for improving cardiovascular efficiency."

Jumping rope is three times as efficient as jogging. And you don't have to go anywhere. Not bad, huh?

IT'S INEXPENSIVE

All you need is a rope, because it's a portable gym. (See Chapter XI for information on just how inexpensive your jumping equipment is.)

IT'S CONVENIENT

You don't need a lot of space or equipment to jump rope. You can jump in any room of your house including your walk-in closet. You don't have to worry about bad weather or nosey neighbors if you consider your exercise program a private matter. And some people do. Take it along with you to work in your purse or briefcase or coat pocket. Jump at the office during coffee break (instead of coffee). It has the same effect: stimulation.

IT'S NOT BORING

Once you become proficient in the program, you can jump while you watch the eggs boil or while you watch television. You can jump to music. If you like nostalgia, jump to some of those old jumping rhymes you used to jump to. Or make up your own.

> "I like coffee, I like tea.
> But this little rope makes a better me."

Or something like that. There is always something new to do with the jump rope. New steps, more speed, jumping with friends. (That's a new one. How'd you like to come over to my place and jump rope!)

IT'S PRACTICAL

You want a simple, quick exercise that conditions as many parts of you as possible, simultaneously. A jump rope fits in a desk drawer much more easily than a set of weights. If you travel, pack the rope instead of a sweat suit. You don't have to worry about jogging on strange streets. Repairs to your "portable gym" are as about as minor as you can get. I haven't worn any out yet. I do tend to lose them like gloves. If you do ever wear one out, you'll be some jumper.

Anytime you feel like jumping . . . you can. Instead of the late evening or early morning "commando raid" on the refrigerator, jump that restlessness off. Except for the gentle whir of the rope, this exercise is noiseless. Your family will appreciate that. Sound far fetched? I've done it to relax and get back to sleep. It *should be noiseless*. It will be noiseless once you've surpassed the beginning awkwardness of the program that everyone feels to some extent, including me. If you begin as I did, hold off on quiet-hour jumping until you are ready. The neighbors won't appreciate that rope slamming on the floor and the thumpty-thump of your still awkward feet pounding. Soon that rope will not touch the floor as it passes beneath your feet. And there will be little sound caused by a pair of soft shoes springing gently a mere inch off the floor and landing again on the balls of the feet.

One way of measuring your technical progress in jumping is by how much or little noise you make.

IT'S SIMPLE

You may find some of the more advanced steps in my program complicated; that is, if you read too far ahead too soon. However, the process of jumping rope itself is very simple. It's a natural exercise for you, because you've been hopping all your life. Remember when your high school team won that close game? Didn't you feel like hopping, jumping up and down with excitement? Such a simple and *natural* function can't be difficult. Jumping rope is easy.

IT'S FUN

I think the idea that a solitary exercise can be fun may be slightly revolutionary. At least, it is to me. There is a joy in knowing your body is growing, turning, developing into what it should be, that you are regaining a lost energy, that your heart and lungs are singing in tune.

There are so many aspects to it. That's fun, too. Physiologically, you can keep a record of your progress by measuring your pulse. You are able to watch yourself grow.

Aesthetically, there is no end to the combinations of steps. Master them all and you will probably look like a ballet dancer doing an Irish jig. Well, that's how it looks to me.

Socially, you are going to surprise some people. Jumping rope, particularly when there are combinations of steps, looks harder than it really is.

After a few weeks, you are hardly aware of how your feet, arms, body and mind have coordinated to give you rope-jumping skills. Others, however, will look at you and say: "How the heck can you do that? How can you jump so long without missing? How come it looks like you're hardly jumping? I can't see your arms moving. Look at that. Looks like a dance." That's fun, too.

Jumping rope strengthens your heart, lungs, legs and wrists. It improves your circulation, firms up breasts, thighs and buttocks. It tones your muscles, improves coordination, improves your skill at sports, reduces nervousness, banishes fatigue, increases endurance, and helps improve your hand-and-foot coordination for everything from dancing and playing the piano (if you play the piano) to driving a car or squeezing through a subway door.

Jumping rope gives you a newfound feeling of well-being that comes from knowing that you and your body are in close harmony with one another, and from *feeling* that harmony. Jumping rope is so simple and natural, it's hard to believe it's an exercise that can do all that. But it can.

It's the fastest-growing exercise in the world. So ask one of the thousands of jumpers about it. It's not hard to find them. They are in dance schools, grade schools, high schools, football and basketball teams, at home, at work, in the back yard, everywhere. Better yet, join them.

V.
What Research Tells Us

As a rope-jumping enthusiast and promoter, I have talked with many people about the exercise and my program. When I talk with other rope-skippers, our conversation centers eventually on the fitness benefits of our exercise and its relative value among the myriad of other exercise activities available.

There is no question that rope skipping improves cardiovascular efficiency, but I want to get down to specifics.

Sometimes, I've worried that maybe a lot of claims about jumping have been exaggerated in an effort to inflate the benefits of rope skipping for commercial reasons: to sell more ropes.

A CHAT WITH DR. JACK BAKER

During my research for this book, I discovered that many rope-skipping promoters have based their claims on some research conducted at Arizona State University by Jack Baker in 1967. Dr. Baker compared rope skipping with jogging under laboratory conditions (as explained in the previous chapter) and concluded that ten minutes of rope skipping could be equated to thirty minutes of jogging. Dr. Baker, now on the faculty of the Physical Education Department at the State University of New York at Buffalo, in conversations with me wished to qualify a few things about his research.

First, Dr. Baker feels his study must be viewed only in its specific context, because it was conducted a decade ago, using primitive testing techniques by today's standards. Dr. Baker advocates the use of rope skipping in fitness-development programs but is hesitant about making any comparisons to other forms of exercise without qualifications.

Therefore, I figured the best thing to do would be to ask Dr. Baker himself to discuss for my readers the available research data on rope skipping.

(Here's Dr. Baker's background, by the way, for interested readers: he received academic degrees from the State University of New York at Brockport, the University of Colorado, and Arizona State University. He has taught physical education and coached at the elementary, junior high, high school and college levels, and for seven years prior to his current appointment, was Director of the Human Performance Laboratory and Director of Adult Fitness Programs at Murray State University.)

Okay, the following is a review of the available research literature concerning rope skipping as compiled by Dr. Baker:

Several articles have been reviewed recommending rope skipping as part of a well-rounded physical activity program.

Rolf E. Melby (1936) claimed that rope skipping benefited organic development, coordination and leg and arm development.

Helen Fahey (1940) indicated that rope skipping promoted rhythm and has masculine appeal. This was in the Kansas City Elementary schools.

Rope skipping supplemented team games and provided maximum exercise in a minimum amount of space in Gordon Hathaway's (1955) program.

Helen Wilber (1966) reported that good body control, improved posture, poise, and balance were the ultimate achievements of rope jumping and that fitness, creativity, skill, challenge and fun were all possible outcomes of this activity. She found rope jumping an appropriate activity applicable to many situations such as classrooms, large or small gymnasiums, and playgrounds.

In his book on rope skipping, Frank Prentup (1963) described the activity as a developer of agility, balance, rhythm and physical condition.

Still, none of the above offered any research evidence that rope skipping was of any benefit to physical fitness.

Marrit Jones, Chadwick Squires and Kaare Rodahl (1962) investigated the effects of a four-week rope skipping program on seven sedentary women between the ages of nineteen and forty-two. The subjects were employees of a large Philadelphia hospital who participated daily in a rope skipping session in which each skipped one minute, rested two minutes for a total of five minutes of skipping and ten minutes of rest. Each subject was tested immediately before and after the experimental four week rope skipping program. Physical work capacity was assessed from the pulse response to submaximal work loads on the bicycle ergometer. After the rope skipping program, the investigators found significant gains in the predicted maximal oxygen intake, and in the pulse response to the submaximal bicycle ergometer work.

It was suggested that rope skipping be adopted as a simple method of improving the physical fitness of a large segment of our population.

Delores Curtis (1963) was interested in the effects of a program of rope skipping on the endurance, leg power, agility, and coordination of elementary school children. A five minute daily period of rope skipping was included in the physical education program of fourth, fifth, and sixth grade children for an eight week period. There were no significant changes in endurance as measured by the vertical jump; in agility as measured by a shuttle run; or in coordination as measured by a test of locomoter coordination. The rope skipping was not detrimental to the children and was suggested as a good activity to keep in the program.

Leg strength and power were the variables in a study that included rope skipping, by Tony Scholnick (1964). Three groups of young men were given tests of leg muscle strength and jumping ability. They then took part in either an isometric or an isotonic strength/power development program. The isotonic program included rope skipping among its four item routine. When compared at the end of the experimental program, it was concluded that there was no difference in the gains in strength and power between the three groups. This study is difficult to analyze, as each of the exercise routines contained more than one type of exercise. Rope skipping could not be isolated.

Physical fitness, as measured by cardiovascular tests, was the center of a study by Joseph Cascino (1964). A program of rope skipping was carried on by ten adult males who ranged in age from nineteen to forty-three. The rope skipping program was conducted five days a week for eight weeks with the subjects working on an individual basis ten minutes each day. Cardiovascular fitness was measured by the use of the Schneider Test, Harvard Step Test, electrocardiogram and physical work capacity as represented by the predicted maximal oxygen uptake. The results of this study indicated that a program of rope skipping would improve the cardiovascular fitness of an adult male. It was further suggested that rope skipping was a comparatively convenient and inexpensive method of promoting circulatory fitness.

Pre-pubescent boys participated in a program where they skipped rope fifteen minutes a day and a half hour on Saturday for a ten week period. A middle-aged man was on a progressive rope skipping program where the length of time spent skipping rope was increased each day. Cascino (1964) reported that cardiovascular fitness improvement resulted from both these programs.

Four approaches to increasing cardiovascular fitness was the substance of a study by Leon Garrett, Muhammad Sabie, and Roy Pangle (1965). The four treatments, each administered during the final three or four minutes of the class period, were running in place, rope skipping, bench stepping, and continued volleyball instruction. From the results it was concluded that cardiovascular fitness increased significantly over the experimental period, but could not be attributed to any single treatment approach.

Rope skipping was compared to calisthenics, isometric exercises, and the regular physical education program for junior high school girls in a study by Florence Ball (1966). After a three month period, it was found that all groups improved, with the calisthenics group showing the greatest improvement, on the motor fitness test. Here again, cardiovascular efficiency was not evaluated.

Audrey Lofgren (1966) compared the effects of one, two and three minute programs of rope skipping on cardiovascular efficiency (as measured by pulse rate recovery) and lower leg strength. One hundred ninth-grade girls were divided into four groups with the experimental subjects skipping one, two, and three minutes respectively, twice weekly for eight weeks. The fourth (control) group did not exercise. It was discovered that all skippers developed leg strength but did not improve their cardiovascular efficiency levels. This study added to the existing knowledge in that bouts of only one, two, or three minutes were to be ineffectual in fitness development.

Baker (1967) compared rope skipping and jogging. Two groups of college men took part in daily programs of thirty minutes of jogging or ten minutes of rope skipping over a six week period. The effects of these programs upon cardiovascular efficiency were evaluated by the Harvard Step Test with each exercise group making marked and nearly equal gains in their levels of cardiovascular fitness. Many rope skipping proponents have used this study to substantiate their claims concerning the benefits of their favorite activity. It must be noted that the instrumentation (testing technique) employed in this study, and other studies up to 1969, lacked the sophistication to render the results conclusive.

A very significant study was conducted by Yoshio Kobayashi at Eastern Illinois University in 1969. This researcher found a marked improvement in the cardiovascular efficiency of high school boys who participated in daily five minute sessions of rope skipping over a period of thirty-five days. The significance of this study lies in the sophistication of the methods of evaluation of cardiovascular efficiency, a factor lacking in all previous research on rope skipping. Kobayashi used a treadmill run and oxygen consumption measurements to evaluate performance. Oxygen consumption techniques are much more reliable than the measuring devices of previous research. A second noteworthy factor is that he gained these results with a daily five-minute exercise bout.

The effects of a ten minute period of rope skipping on elements of physical fitness and badminton skill was studied by Sheila Donaghe (1963). Subjects were administered a fitness test consisting of squat-thrusts, toe-touches, curl-ups, pull-ups and an agility run in addition to a badminton skill achievement test. All subjects received badminton instruction with half the group taking part in a daily ten-minute rope skipping program. The researcher claimed that the rope skipping group improved in fitness, but no more so than the non-skipping group. It should be noted, however, that the fitness test items included do not evaluate cardiovascular efficiency. A secondary conclusion drawn from this study states that rope skipping had no measurable effect upon badminton skill.

Fencing instruction was supplemented with rope skipping in a study by Barbara Franklin in 1966. This researcher discovered that rope skipping aided in the development of wrist flexibility and wrist extension strength, two attributes of a successful fencer. The improvements were slight, however, and rope skipping has not become a routine phase of fencing training.

Exercises and exercise promoters are constantly making comparisons between various forms of activity. The Baker study equated ten minutes of rope skipping with thirty minutes of jogging; others make comparisons to sports activities such as golf and tennis, while still other writers make comparisons to other recognized fitness programs.

In the development of his concept of "Aerobic Exercise," Cooper (1968 & 1970) studied many exercise forms in an attempt to understand their general and specific physical fitness benefits. Through his Aerobic Point System, we are able to make activity comparisons that can help us understand the relative worth of various activities in the development of cardiovascular fitness.

Referring to the Cooper chart, we can equate ten minutes of continuous rope skipping with running one mile in twelve minutes, cycling two miles in six minutes, swimming a quarter of a mile in twelve minutes, twenty minutes of handball, two sets of tennis, and eighteen holes of golf. Fifteen minutes of continuous rope skipping compares to running one mile in eight minutes, cycling four miles in thirteen minutes, swimming a quarter of a mile in eight minutes, thirty minutes of handball, three sets of tennis, and twenty-seven holes of golf. It should be noted, however, that, even with Cooper's "Aerobic Point System," these comparisons are approximate, at best, as many individual differences enter into the fitness picture.

The important relationship in these comparisons is the time factor. No researcher or fitness director can make precise time-factor/activity-relationship comparisons. We can deduce, however, that rope skipping *is* a valid cardiovascular exercise, *and* that the exercise time period is less than that required in most instances.

In summary, the research data indicate that rope skipping is a worth-while activity for the development of muscular strength and endurance, cardiovascular fitness, balance, agility, and coordination. It is an activity that requires only one, inexpensive, piece of equipment and has virtually no specialized space requirements. Rope skipping's paramount asset appears to be its relative short time commitment for derived benefits.

ADDITIONAL RESEARCH

In addition to Dr. Baker's compendium, here are some additional studies as compiled by *Physical Fitness Research Digest*, published by the President's Council on Physical Fitness and Sports.

Nikki Assman, for her master's thesis at the University of Wisconsin-Lacrosse, in 1969, tested twenty-eight coeds in rope skipping, jogging, running and control, five days per week for eight weeks. The jumpers started with one minute of skipping, followed by thirty seconds' rest, until they had jumped for a total of ten minutes. Eventually, they skipped continuously for the full ten minutes at 125 turns per minute. The joggers worked up to thirty minutes of continuous jogging. The runners gradually were able to run a mile in seven minutes.

All three groups were tested for circulatory-respiratory endurance. Rope-skippers showed the greatest improvement of 15 percent, as compared to nearly 10 percent for the runners and nearly 4 percent for the joggers.

John Powel, in his graduate thesis at the University of Illinois in 1957, studied rope-skipping effects on five ten-year-old boys who skipped five days each week for ten weeks. They performed as many skips as possible in without missing, did as many turns as possible in five successive efforts, and performed as many skips as possible in sixty seconds. In 1964, Joseph Cascino applied the same test to men between the ages of 19 and 43 in his thesis at Temple University. Both the Powel and the Cascino groups showed improvement in leg and knee strength, faster running speed, greater agility and flexibility, broader shoulders and deeper chests, and improved heart response. Cascino's group showed an overall gain in endurance of 25 percent.

Sondra Wattenbarger tested the effects of pacing on heart rates during rope jumping for her master's thesis at Oklahoma State University in 1969 with 187 junior high school girls as subjects. A rope-skipping test, consisting of the number of skips performed in two minutes, was administered as part of a physical fitness testing program. The subjects were then retested, using a cadence provided by a metronome. The girls had significantly more skips on the paced test and had significantly lower heart rates at the end of the paced test as compared to the unpaced test. Those classified as skilled rope-skippers had significantly lower heart rates at the end of skipping than those classified as unskilled performers.

In summary, *Physical Fitness Research Digest* noted these factors must be present in exercise for cardiovascular improvement:

Exercise should be adapted to the individual's exercise tolerance.
Reasonable overloading should be applied to induce a higher level of performance.
The exercise plan should be progressive.
Sedentary adults especially should receive medical clearance before embarking on a vigorous exercise program.

The same activities may be used effectively to improve circulatory-respiratory endurance and to reduce fat.

Several investigators compared rope skipping to other physical activities with results such as the following: With the Harvard Step Test as the evaluative instrument, college men showed comparable improvement from rope skipping ten minutes a day and from jogging 30 minutes daily, five days a week for six weeks.

Similar results were obtained with college women as subjects when rope skipping was contrasted with jogging and with running, but with Cooper's twelve-minute run/walk test as the evaluative instrument.

Three groups of college women were contrasted when participating in rope skipping, jogging and aerobic dancing, with each period being twelve minutes in duration and all exercise sessions regulated to heart rates between 140 and 150 beats per minute; all three groups made comparable gains in maximum oxygen intake, and the rope-skipping group improved more than the other two groups in lean body mass.

Of significance, too, are the control factors that are important in effective rope skipping, including the length of time skipping is continued, the interspersing of rest periods between skipping, and the rapidity of the rope turns. In other words, a paced program, a plan, is essential.

VI.
Jumping For Health

Can five-to-ten minutes of jumping rope a day really put you into a state of perfect health?

Okay, first, what is health? Health is freedom from disease. You don't have to be healthy to be fit. More than once, top atheletes have set and broken records while suffering from a cold or flu.

One day, I visited a local pet shop and noticed a magnificent painting of a young cheetah, the fastest animal in the world, hanging above the cash register. As I gazed at what could be nature's most perfect combination of strength, endurance and agility, I asked about the cat. "He was our 'pet,'" the owner replied. "But he died at less than a year old." I paused to fantasize having a cheetah for a household pet before I asked, "What happened?"

"Heart attack," the owner sighed.

Heart attack! What could be stronger than the heart of the world's fastest creature? What a rare stroke of misfortune. A fluke. An act of God.

I can't lead you to a state of *perfect* health. I can't even bring you health at all. I *can* help you become *physically fit* with a minimum of effort and time.

And fitness increases tremendously your odds of being and staying healthy.

Fitness is the capacity of your body to perform work. Your level of fitness is your level of work capacity. If you are fit, your capacity of energy is more than sufficient to meet the demands of life with your back, legs, arms, heart, lungs, and mind. You are not just technically healthy, you are as healthy as you can get. You have energy potential. Not the store of energy, really, but the capacity to supply energy.

Right now, you know you are not fit. You feel it. You feel your weakness, your lack of energy, your physical flabbiness. You may be fatigued, listless, bored, stressed. And you're ready to do something about it. That's good. Because if you don't do something about your physical condition, your life is possibly going to be shorter in quantity and certainly in quality.

The American male ranks only 17th in longevity among men of the major nations of the world. American women rank tenth. American women, however, die of heart diseases more often than women from any other country. That death rate is increasing, and at an earlier age.

In 1900, heart disease accounted for only 14 percent of the deaths in the United States. Today, more than half the deaths are attributed to cardiovascular disease. The major causes of death in men 35 to 54 years of age are all to some extent preventable: heart disease, lung cancer, automobile accidents, cirrhosis of the liver and stroke. Dr. Kenneth Cooper of *Aerobics* fame, philosophizes: How many of these are acts of God and how many of these are acts of men?

These factors affect your health; heredity, smoking, drinking, obesity, poor diet, and lack of exercise. We don't wear out, we rust out.

Exercise with my jump program and improve your diet. You can lose weight jumping rope. My program helps you relax and feel better mentally. Such stress reduction could cut down your alcohol intake. You may feel so in tune with your body that you actually quit smoking. That leaves only heredity to contend with.

You see, I want you to do more than jump rope. Jumping produces a joy about activity that affects you continually. Right now, that feeling of not wanting to do something exerting like jumping a fence or taking the stairs is your mind's response to an unfit body. If your body were fit, your mind would know it and say, "I bet I could jump that fence," or, "Let's take the stairs. It feels good." You and I have been looking for the easy way out for too long. I recall a cartoon in the *New Yorker* magazine depicting two businessmen standing on a downtown street in Manhattan. One is saying to the other: "Should we walk or do we have time to take a cab?" A joke about traffic and a comment on a sedentary way of life.

You are sedentary. Awful-sounding word, isn't it? It's not your fault, really. Your job keeps your physical activity at a minimum. The stress of your work, the other challenges of life cause you to seek comfort whenever and wherever you can find it. Comfort like the elevator, the escalator, the chair, the couch, the car, and the bed.

It is going to be difficult for you to accept vigorous exercise as an effective way to relieve *fatigue*, for example. But it does, and we'll discuss more about it later.

The point is, inactivity is not really an easy way of life. It was once believed that physical acitivity added to the wear and tear on the body tissues and advanced the aging process. We know now that the opposite is true. Body tissues and functions are improved by the right exercise.

Life is not all work. Work is a means to an end: enjoyment of life. But your body was designed to work. It thrives on work. Its efficiency is measured by the amount of work it has to do.

When the work load is reduced, muscles waste away, and strength is lost. The body becomes less able to meet physical demands and may fail in emergency situations. For example, the weak body may be unable to cope with even a mild heart attack.

According to Dr. Alexander Leaf of the Harvard Medical School, lack of activity at any age causes the loss of calcium salts in our bones. They become thin and fragile, just as muscles atrophy and become smaller and weaker with disuse. Astronauts sent into orbit for the first week-long trip in space lost 10 percent of their bone during that time. Nowadays, astronauts exercise while in space.

The President's Council on Physical Fitness states that there is "strong authoritative support for the concept that regular exercise can help prevent degenerative disease and slow down the physical deterioration that accompanies aging. Individuals who engage in proper physical activity have better job performance records, fewer degenerative diseases and probably a longer life expectancy than the population at large."

Aging. The war against gravity. What would it be worth to you to be independent as long as you live? To be able to take care of yourself without the help of anyone else? To come and go with freedom? To feel well and look well? What would it be worth to know that your later years can be as full of activity, interest, and enjoyment as your youth and middle age?

Again, from the President's Council: "The fitness challenge in later years is the mortal enemy of the human body. We know today that *how* a person lives, not how *long* he lives, is responsible for many of the physical problems associated with advanced age." You can do nothing about your chronological age. But you can do something about your physiological age.

We are witnessing a great period of physiological research, most of which seems to deny "the great lie," as Dr. Irene Gore called it in her book, *Add Years to Your Life and Life to Your Years*: "The great lie perpetrated on the middle-aged and older that the human body is like a machine . . . that it runs down, wears out and eventually stops functioning, like a machine." We know now that the opposite is true. Possibly, rather than being a lie, the earlier attitude was fostered by ignorance.

The facts as we know them now are that while machines do wear out from use, bodies thrive on it. Decline in age is not due to years, but to disease, mental and physical inactivity, and even laziness.

What does that mean, then, to the older person? It means that the physiological aging process is guided by the level of physical activity in our lives. Proper exercise by young and old results in similar relative increases in muscular strength and working capacity.

It means that age is measured not by years, but by the physiological potential of the individual, and that is the way medical authorities respond to it.

It means we know less about the aging process than we even thought.

It means that it's not how long you live that's important, but how alive you are while you live.

As Dr. Rodahl explains, in sedentary people there is a gradual decrease of physical work capacity after age 20. The maximum work capacity of an inactive man at 75 is only about half that of a boy of 17. But in a *well-trained, physically fit* older individual, the decline in physical work capacity is very small. An older, unfit person has the potential to improve his work capacity to a level within 15 percent of what he had as a hearty 20-year-old! *If he exercises.*

A fit 65-year-old man may be superior in physical capacity to an unfit 35-year-old man!

Say good-bye to one of the greatest cop-outs of all time by the unfit: "Well, I guess I'm just getting old."

Yes, of course, biological aging takes place. Activity lessens in glands and organs, hair coloring is lost, cell connective tissue weakens and so on. And that's why physical and mental activity becomes more important the older you are.

I am not suggesting you should jump rope in your seventies . . . just because I happen to know a 68-year-old grandmother who does. Definitely not. Your physician will advise you. I am, however, showing you what the facts are in regard to physical acitivity to prolong and improve your life, no matter what age you are. You can no longer say: "I'm too old for that."

Recently, I read of research underway for what has been termed: "The Death Hormone." Now that we know that the body does not wear out, the question is: What does happen?

Suppose the heredity factor were set aside in the question of longevity and we considered an individual who was theoretically at the peak of fitness. He won't live forever. Theories have it now that the pituitary gland may release an end-it-all hormone once the brain decides the individual's procreative purposes are completed. It has been determined that such an event takes place in other living creatures. Salmon, for example.

Optimistic scientists surmise that isolating such a hormone in man, if it does exist, could prolong our life span to an average of 150 to 200 years.

I've discussed this prospect with friends. The consensus is, "Boy, who would want to live that long!" Again, it's the quality, not the quantity of life that should concern us. Independence, interest, joy, activity, stimulation, action, movement, health, *fitness* . . . is life. Not, twenty, fifty or seventy years on the calendar.

You and I can become fit at any age. Vitality is not confined to youth. Vitality is agelessness. When you think of vitality, think of fitness. This fitness, this vitality, this energy cannot be stored. It must be acquired constantly throughout life through exercise. And it must be used. Use it or lose it.

We have a choice about how we should age. Exercise delays the aging process. Exercise strenghthens the heart, the bones, all of our organs, including your sexual ones.

The right kind of exercise buys years. An inactive life is a form of slow suicide. The fountain of youth is right inside your body.

There may be no definite clinical proof yet that exercise prolongs life, but there is definitely no evidence whatever that exercise hurts life. Instead, there is a huge amount of data which indicates exercise enhances our chances of living longer and living better.

We do know that aging is accelerated by inactivity, and lack of exercise seems to be a factor in premature aging. If you are 26 or beyond, pay attention because you are at that point in your life where the biological aging process begins.

Medical research also demonstrates that active persons have fewer heart attacks than sedentary persons. If they do suffer attacks, they recover more rapidly and easily. If you are over 40, pay attention because it would be best to preserve your arteries above all else. Arteries are the canals that keep blood flowing to the heart and brain.

Pick up any health book. It will have a chapter or chapters on exercise. If it doesn't, put it back down. You can find what I have just outlined for you on the benefits of exercise for better health in dozens of books. I'd like you to explore other materials on health and exercise besides this one. These will help you when and if you get discouraged during your exercise program. If you say, "What was I doing this for again?" I want you to remember well.

Actually, you probably have a pretty good idea that exercise is good for you or you wouldn't have gone this far with me. You may, however, have discovered just how valuable the *right kind* of exercise is for you in the quantity and quality of your life.

Once you begin jumping, I don't want you to stop, ever. Remember, your motivation for jumping may be to lose weight or reduce stress or improve your body or to help your golf swing, but primarily, you are jumping for health. Can you think of a better joy?

VII.
Jumping for Sex

Two friends were talking. One said to the other, "A strange thing has been happening to me. Every time I sneeze, I become sexually aroused."

"Really," said the other. "That is strange. What are you taking for it?"

The first replied: "Oh, pepper."

Well, practice makes perfect. Isn't that the old saying?

Let's face it. Performance in bed, both in quantity and quality, depends on sensuality and energy. Some have compared the sex experience to the mile run in terms of energy expenditure. If you're fatigued and flabby, you'll respond accordingly.

Sex is in part a strength and endurance situation. Demands are made on your nervous and cardiovascular systems. Some sexual postures cause a certain amount of muscular fatigue. The heart rate and blood pressure goes up. Timing is important during a sexual experience. Your timing is off if you find you must stop what you're doing to "catch your breath."

How you regard yourself can affect your sex life, too. If you feel flabby, out-of-shape and unappealing, you'll send that message to your partner. There will be no sensuality.

Conversely, if you look in the mirror and see forgotten muscles becoming firm and filling out, the belly flat again, hips, thighs and buttocks trim, you're going to like what you see. And if you like what you see, you're more willing to have others look at you, touch you. That's sex appeal. It's never available to anyone else unless you see it first.

Jumping rope will give you more out of life sexually. You'll look a little younger and feel better. And you'll know it.

Laurence Morehouse cites a test of older people in his book *Total Fitness*. Studies were done on residents of Leisure World in Southern California. Results indicated exercise lessened the depressive states often found in older people. Those with higher fitness scores also reported a more satisfactory sexual life in their later years.

This feeling of well-being which results from the exercise of rope jumping is important to the quality of your sex life. Tension and stress from life's frustrations can deter your sexual interest and ability. Sex relieves tension. The problem is getting your mind off of what was making you tense long enough to have sex. That isn't as easy as it sounds sometimes.

Exercise is a natural way to relieve tension. Just jump. The physical experience will relax you naturally.

Dr. Rodahl performed an experiment among married airmen in Alaska in which a group of them were required to spend several weeks in the wilderness in midwinter on a simulated survival exercise. For three weeks, they were forced to keep vigorously active just in order to survive. As a result, they became physically fit for the first time in their lives. When they returned, those most pleasantly surprised with the change in the men were their wives.

Of course, there may be other complications or problems that are affecting your experience in bed which can't be alleviated by my exercise program. All I can tell you is the heightened vitality and improved appearance created by this program will heighten your sensuality and sexual response to the point where you may even find yourself leaving the light on!

Fitness enhances all of life's activities at any age. And, again, "I'm getting too old," cannot be justified as a reason for decline in sexual activity until the very later years of your life, and maybe not even then. Lack of fitness, of vitality, of energy production, however, can effect a decline in your sex life, just as the absence of these qualities can cause a decline in all other aspects of your life.

VIII.
The Stress Factor

On the surface, the thought of jumping rope to help your sex life may seem a little silly. But I wouldn't let anything stand in the way of a good sex life if I could help it, would you?

Frankly, I have to admit that the best form of relaxation I know of is sex. It's even better than jumping rope. It requires no special equipment and costs nothing. Stress can be relieved by sex. Lack of sex causes stress. But one well-known physical effect of stress is a lowering of your sex drive. Now, we have a paradox.

If sex relieves tension but you are too tense to have sex, you're in a pickle. That's enough to make anybody "hopping mad." So go ahead and hop. Jump and relax.

It has been suggested that social stress can act as a kind of population control. Animals placed in crowded conditions breed less. It's likely that humans are affected the same way.

Studies have shown that people usually find their sexual capacity improves on holidays when they are away from the stresses of work and the crowded life in towns. Stress is probably one of the most potent contraceptives of the modern world. Stress is also a killer and a maimer.

I'm influenced easily. When I watch a television commercial which asks me if I have the pain of headache, I sometimes get the pain of headache. So I have to be careful with this chapter. I don't want you to feel stress after reading it.

Optimism can be a great deterrent to stress. If you feel defeated because you feel unfit, my jump rope program will help you. You don't need to feel more defeated just thinking of fitness programs you want to try but can't handle. Possibly, you already feel guilty about not being strong enough to pick up the gauntlet of rigorous exercise. That's stress.

As the Greeks understood so well, the mind and the body cannot really be separated. Train your body and you are on the road to training your mind and your psyche. Developing "nerves of steel" is part of becoming fit. Build the equipment you need to cope with stress. Stress. An optimist would call it "life's little challenges."

Medical science measures fitness in terms of one's ability to tolerate stress, the struggles of life. You may consider stress your enemy. Actually, your true enemy is unfitness. Stress, on the other hand, is more fickle. Stress can become either your ally or your enemy's ally. Stress joins the winner. If you are fit, stress will be on your side. If you are unfit . . . you've got double trouble.

One of the problems in coping with stress is, paradoxically, that the body and mind are built to thrive on stress. Stress is pushing and shoving, action and reaction. Stress is stimulation. In fact, some people like stress. Some people work better under pressure. Some people like to jump out of airplanes, go off ski jumps, and race cars. Some people seem to enjoy emotional trauma. Some people thrive on deadlines, yet others are frustrated by the job yet to be done, the hill yet to be climbed, the money yet to be made. They seem to like challenge, even trauma, or trouble. I've heard them referred to as "crisis-oriented," people who cannot perform unless there is pressure, unless there is a crisis situation.

That's fine as long as there is relief. When challenge permeates your total life, total work, total play, there is trouble. Long term high-level stress has physical effects that can be fatal. A permanent high heart rate and blood pressure can cause heart attacks, which are perhaps the most common result of excess tension, and stress.

Addiction to drugs is not limited to those chemicals introduced externally. The body produces some of the most powerful drugs available in terms of altering and controlling the human system. You can become addicted to your own adrenaline. An overdose, prompted by continual, high-level stress conditions, can be fatal.

Another problem in coping with stress is the lack of awareness of the battle your body is fighting to cope. Have you ever been in an auto accident that almost was? At the time, it's all instinct. Your body is numb, concentrated on reacting to the situation. You swerve, hit the brakes and escape a perilous situation. Then, when the danger has passed, you feel your heart pounding, your mouth drying and your tongue thickening. As your pulse races, you feel as though you were on an elevator that stopped too suddenly. Only then, afterward, are you truly aware of the stress put upon your body and mind.

Your own body released powerful doses of drugs into itself to aid in coping with a situation that spelled danger. All on its own. You didn't have to think and say, "Oh, trouble. Do something." Your body did it automatically.

It's as if your body and mind had mobilized for war. Headquarters, the brain, alerted the hormone squads to disperse immediately. Your heart rate raised, pumping more blood to the muscles. Your lungs provided more oxygen, and sugar and fat reserves were released. Each time stress is applied, your body mobilizes for fight or flight. You used extra energy uncontrollably. Just imagine what happens when your energy-producing potential is low, when you are unfit.

To understand the erosive capabilities of undue stress, consider the simple analogy of the accelerating and braking system of your car. The sympathetic and parasympathetic nervous systems of your body work the same way.

Your accelerating chemical is called sympathin. It helps you cope with tense situations like a confrontation with a mugger, equipment that doesn't work, telephone calls, unpaid bills, ingratitude, divorce, and taxes. When the crisis is over, your body applies the brakes with acetylcholine.

You know how constant acceleration and braking can wear your car's engine. You can also drown from a flood of chemicals to your sympathetic nerve endings.

Everyday we must cope with flashing lights, ringing bells, roaring motors, yelling voices, screeching tires and penetrating smells. Stress can be everything from asking for a raise to not getting those front row center seats you wanted.

Recently, much more has been learned about the effects of mental stress on the body. It can cause physical symptoms of all kinds, from acne to impotence.

Half the beds in American hospitals are occupied by mental patients. *Medical authorities are wondering how many of those patients could have coped with stress more adequately by being physically fit.*

As a matter of fact, it is no longer a question of physical fitness or medical fitness or, for that matter, spiritual, social, or moral fitness. It is a question of just plain "fitness," an all-encompassing word which refers to a general state of well-being.

Researchers have even discovered that people whose names start from S to Z die sooner than those whose names begin from A to R. The reason? More frustration, probably. All their lives, the S to Z people have had to wait longer in line. Another kind of stress.

Physical stress, no matter what you do all day, is always present. Sitting at a desk takes twice as much energy as does resting. If the work load requires an energy output which is greater than one-third of your peak working capacity, you are going to be tired at the end of an eight-hour day.

Illness itself can be a kind of stress that affects patients differently, depending on their general fitness. What might result in the common cold to the fit person could stimulate a spiral of hard-to-fight germs invading the unfit body.

Emotional stress, the fight-or-flight mechanism, is primitive. You can't tell your boss to take a walk in the lake until his hat floats, or bite the ear of the person in front of you who just stepped on your toe in the elevator. Nor is honking at red lights a satisfying method of relieving emotional stress. Emotional stress can harm the ineffective body that can't adapt to the strain.

Having a fit body in itself is no guarantee, of course, of emotional well-being, but if you're going to take the trouble to put your body in shape, stay trim and energetic, you are just naturally going to feel better about yourself than someone who lets his or her body go to pot. You are going to feel better about yourself. That extra self-esteem may be enough self-assurance to stop worrying about yourself as much.

Some words about fatigue. Fatigue, insomnia, chronic tiredness may be symptoms of organic disease. Only your physician can tell you for sure. But many people become fatigued because of the lack of physical activity.

Physical fatigue combined with sleeplessness is often an indicator of lack of exercise. Ironically, then, the cure for fatigue and restlessness may not be more rest but the right kind of physical activity. Physical, emotional, psychological and mental fatigues are all states in which you owe your body more oxygen than you are giving it.

The highly trained long-distance runner can be physically exhausted at the end of the race. He used more energy than he was providing. He exceeded the limits of his exertion capabilities.

The corporate executive can be fatigued after sitting at a desk all day, taking the elevator to the underground garage, driving home and flopping on the couch. He went *under* his exertion level. His muscles did not work to supply him with enough oxygen to maintain a minimum oxygen-consuming level. He rests because he's tired; result: he gets more tired.

Fatigue is a big part of our conversations. "I'm tired of this and I'm tired of that. I'm depressed." Actually, the word is deflated. Deprived of air.

So inflate. Get sick and tired of being sick and tired. Hop to it.

You have three weapons with which to cope with stress.

First, the number of stressful situations in your life are a factor. So don't encourage them. Avoid exposing yourself to crises. Don't look for them. Plan ahead, try to avoid them if possible. Of course, life is still full of pitfalls.

Secondly, your personality determines just how much or how little you react to stress.

Third, your life-style affects the capacity of your body to resist stress. Combine all three, then, with a new special attitude about your body and mind. Be aware that your involuntary system is going to trigger against stress with the same intensity, no matter what shape your mind and body are in. Develop enough strength to supply the demands your system will make.

The right exercise can expand your ability to cope. Physical fitness can make you less neurotic, more imaginative and more independent.

So try getting the clutter out of your life and off the top of your desk. If you have three things to do, do only one. If you exercise, don't compete with anyone, including yourself, until you are ready. Am I saying, take time to "smell the roses?" Yes. Start trying to stay alive. Take time to be human.

Don't get me wrong. I don't want you to sit down. I want you to realize that if it's the right exercise, you can find relaxation in physical activity. I want you to move in a manner that is not only sensuous and natural, but is calculated, paced and controlled.

Hopping or jumping is a natural way of moving, especially under stress conditions. My program will help you channel and calculate that hop into a simple fitness program.

Any weekend afternoon during the football season will give evidence of the human habit of hopping to relieve tension. Players jump up and down in the end zone. Cheerleaders leap about. The crowd jumps to their feet.

Watch a daytime television money show. When a contestant wins, he or she jumps up and down. Jumping to blow off steam is even part of our language. We become "hopping mad," say "jumping Jimminy," and "jumping Jehoshaphat." We even "jump for joy."

Jumping will restore your heart, legs, and lungs to cope with stress. Fitness will change your personality and make you more self-assured and more self-sufficient. You'll have a new feeling of well-being and be more willing to accept demanding challenges.

Bringing your body to maximum efficiency will free your mind and emotions to do their best. You will find yourself living more comfortably with the human unease that often obsesses all of us.

That's the joy of jumping.

IX.
Lighten the Load

Getting in shape to you may mean getting your shape in shape. The idea that jumping rope can firm and trim you and get rid of inches may have been the main reason you picked up this book.

Suddenly, you have flab. You can feel it jiggle when your car hits a bump in the road. The way you look doesn't make you feel good. Or the way you feel doesn't make you look good. You realize that dieting or exercise alone isn't going to get you where you want to be soon enough. It takes a combination of the right diet and the right exercise to be at your proper weight and proper proportions.

You do not necessarily have to be fat to be flabby. As furniture movers know, the key to carrying a load easily is weight distribution.

Let's find out where you are. First, I want you to ignore the scale and look in the mirror. Look at your waistline. Men have a rather constant and uniform body construction and, consequently, a fairly uniform distribution of fat throughout their bodies. Men, look toward the center of gravity, generally in the area of the stomach. If there is flab or excess fat, that area continues around the sides to what I've heard referred to affectionately as "love handles."

Women, on the other hand, have contours, and I, for one, am grateful for that. Ladies have no regularity of fat distribution. It can gather around the thighs or buttocks or breasts or upper arms. Women can stay thin on top and become fat on the bottom.

Try a couple of tests. The first is called the "pinch test." Reach up near the tricep or underarm and pinch about one quarter to a half-inch of your fat layer. (Everybody has a fat layer.) If you find an excess, you have excess fat. You have work to do. Try it on the abdomen. You shouldn't gather more than an inch to remain within the normal. An inch of pinch means about forty pounds of fat in most adults. That's okay. Fat comprises about 40 percent of the weight of a normal adult.

Now, let's try another test. Lie down with a yardstick. Place the yardstick over your abdomen so one end rests on your chest and the other end on your pelvic bone. Take a look. Does it form a bridge over your abdomen or does it teeter in mid-air because its middle is elevated by your stomach? The latter means it's time to work.

Here's another test. Measure your waistline and add your waist size in inches to the number 36.

That is called your fat index and you can compare the index to your height in inches. Your fat index should be the same as or less than your height. For every inch your fat index is above your height, you are 2½ percent over your ideal weight.

What you see in the mirror may be initially of more value than what you see on the scale, because you can actually lose weight and gain fat. Athletes find themselves with this phenomenon at the end of a season. They stop working out, but keep eating the same amount. Their muscles atrophy. But muscles weigh more than fat, so the loss in muscles shows up as a loss of weight on the scale. The scale tells little about fat.

Or suppose you weigh yourself the morning after you ate four pounds of food. You show a gain of three pounds. If you wait three days until all the food is processed in your body, those three pounds will be gone.

Your body absorbs moisture on humid days to such an extent that your scale weight could increase by as much as a pound and a half. The object of weight reduction is to lose excess fat without reducing the lean tissues of your body. You may gain weight, but one look in the mirror should tell the story. You look firm, trim, flat in the right places and not so flat in the other places. That's our goal.

An aquaintance bragged to me that he has been able to maintain the same body weight for over twenty years without regular exercise and diet. He didn't realize that because of limited activity, his body composition may have changed. That muscle tissue he had when he was younger may have been supplanted by fat. He may have the same body weight, but not the most healthy distribution. In the case of your body, you can't tell the contents by weighing the package. Even though my friend's weight is constant and within standards, he's not really acknowledging what he sees in the mirror. His body structure may be such that fat deposits are not obvious when he is standing still. But a few short hops in front of the mirror may tell another story. Flab bounces. So don't be fooled by the scale.

One who maintains a constant weight and shape is a rare bird. Odds are, you are slightly overweight or have too much fat in the wrong places, or both. Women have a worse problem keeping everything in its proper place than men do.

As I mentioned earlier, you as a woman may have a battle going on in the outer thigh area and lower buttocks as well as the abdomen and upper arms. Rope skipping offers a one-two punch by burning calories which trim you and exercising muscles in the problem areas which shape you.

My jump-rope program will not change your shape. You are stuck with that. But the right kind of exercise program can change your appearance.

Some people are endomorphic: round shoulders, wide hips, short neck. Others are ectomorphic: tall, long fingers and neck, thin. Still others are mesomorphic: broad shoulders and narrow hips, triangular-shaped. I can't convert you from an endomorph to an ectomorph. Neither can anyone else. But I can help you be the best you can be and look the best you are able to look.

First of all, you must lighten the load. Twenty-five percent of America is at least fifteen pounds overweight. And fifty million of us suffer from obesity.

Obesity is bad. A man 20 percent overweight increases his chance for an early death by 20 percent. Fat people commit suicide more often, have more accidents, more heart attacks, more bladder disease, more arthritis (probably, from carrying a heavy load) more backaches. Fat people take 4,300 extra breaths a day. Their heart beats ten times more per minute.

With every extra pound of fat, miles of new blood vessels are needed which draw blood away from other body organs unnecessarily and place a strain on the heart.

For a middle-aged man, each pound of overweight means an increased chance of premature death of about one percent. If you weigh ten to twenty pounds over your ideal body weight, you are overweight. If you are thirty pounds over that ideal, you are obese.

Actually, we've been a little too gentle with ourselves. We get on the scale, and as the needle zooms, we say: "Ooops. Looks like I have to lose some weight." No, it looks like you have to lose some *fat*. "Weight" is the polite word for "fat," which we use to temper the fact that we are overabundant in that substance. You are going to embark on a *fat* loss program. Think of it that way. Don't just think of weight, but what it is that weighs: *Fat*. Keep it to yourself, of course. Going up to a friend and saying: "Hey, looks like you've lost some *fat*!" probably would hurt his or her feelings. For yourself, however, face the facts: You are not slightly overweight or out of shape. You have too much *fat*.

Whether you are slightly over-fat, obese, or even at your ideal weight, if you have flab, you have too much fat. It hasn't been easy for you to get rid of, right? Among other problems in losing fat, there are the complications of social pressure, the presence of those skinny people who never gain weight, and being in too much of a hurry to get off the flab in the right way.

Social pressure. Sharing of food is often a significant event. There is unity and friendship in sharing a feast. We tend to eat more than we really want to while "breaking bread" with friends, customers, and neighbors. Leisure invites fatness. Physical inactivity leads to increased food intake. People overeat because they're depressed, because they're unhappy. People eat the wrong kinds of foods because of speed and convenience. There are dozens of reasons why we take on fat that can be blamed on our social environment.

Health authorities are constantly arguing over which foods are right for you and which aren't, bombarding us with more and more complicated plans to receive proper nutrition. It's enough to make you give up listening and go have a cookie. And watch television. Or just sit there.

And what about those people who never seem to gain weight no matter how much they eat. They don't help either. Makes you think you have a special problem that causes weight gain. "I'm just naturally chubby." "Well, I'm big-boned, you know." The odds that you have a medical problem are small. Your doctor can be the judge of that.

There is a mystery, however, as to why people get fat. Some people are able to maintain constant body weight without thinking about how much food they eat or the amount of exercise they take. And there is no evidence that all fat people necessarily eat that much more than thin people. It is believed that some folks are more efficient at converting food energy to body tissue due to a variance in their basic metabolism rate. Some people are just easy gainers.

Those lucky skinny people who can eat anything they want are not necessarily fit and may still be fat. Again, it's not always how much you weigh, but how much of you is fat. Strange as it sounds, there are fat skinny people.

When you consider the amount of food the average adult consumes in a lifetime, thirty-five tons, it's amazing how little body weight fluctuates. If there were a one percent error in the balance between food intake and energy expenditure, body weight would theoretically double for some people every twenty years. Yet most adults fluctuate in weight by only a few kilos (ten or twelve pounds) in their lifetime.

So, you say, "Oh, no. I've got fat. I've got to get rid of it fast." You're in a hurry. And some enterprisers have cashed in on your anxiety with "crash" diets. It appears easier to you. Suffer dearly for a short time and get it over with. The results of fast weight loss are temporary. Remember the smoker who said: "I know I can quit. I've done it dozens of times." The "crash" dieter says: "I know I can lose weight. I've done it dozens of times."

Not only does it not last—losing weight in a hurry can be harmful. You may not loose fat. You may lose protein. Body tissue. A severe caloric restriction may cause protein to be mobilized from your muscles, including your heart muscles, in order to supply the needed energy for your body. Rapid weight loss can make you tired and irritable.

The only way to lose weight, fat, permanently and safely is slowly. Slowly and sensibly. But it's also the easy way.

Choose a weight you wish to stay at for the rest of your life. Strive toward that ideal weight by reducing only a pound a week. Anything more rapid may have detrimental side effects. Anything more rapid stands a good chance of not lasting.

Fats, proteins, carbohydrates, vitamins, and minerals are all essential to your well-being. Anytime you take on a "special" diet that calls for the elimination of any kind of food element without personal medical advice, you are inviting trouble.

You need all the nutrients available in food. Protein is the brick and mortar of your body. It builds tissue and repairs injuries and wear and tear. Our flesh and blood are proteins. So are the enzymes that carry out the digestive processes, the digestive tract itself, even our hair, fingernails, and some hormones.

An adult loses and needs to replace about forty grams of protein a day.

Carbohydrates appear in each living cell minutely and compose only 1½ percent of the body. Carbohydrates are the body's first source of energy. When fuel is needed, first fire goes to "carbos."

Vitamins are not food. They are catalysts. Mixed with the food in your body, vitamins cause things to happen. Normally, we have enough vitamin A in our body to meet our requirements for two years, enough vitamin B^{12} for ten. We have enough of even the most rapidly depleted vitamins, thiamin and vitamin C, to meet our needs for more than two months.

And because we may have been a little rough on fat, it's especially important that we examine its function. Fat dissolves certain vitamins so they can enter the bloodstream and supply insulation for frayed nerve cells. Fat cells in the body are storage bins of food intake and remain there for emergencies. In the time when man hunted for food and found it irregularly, fat was an essential emergency food supply. Today, food is regularly available. Thus, the problem. Fat is high-octane fuel for your body engine. If there is a tremendous energy demand, the body burns carbohydrates first, then fat, and finally, protein.

We want to burn the right amount of fat, the right amount of energy, while maintaining our normal metabolic rate. Fat burns while protein is preserved. Ideally, you want to lose a pound of excess fat while not losing a pound of water or a pound of vital body tissue.

Sixty percent of your body is water. That percentage is necessary to maintain normal function of tissues. We can only afford to lose 10 percent of our water. Because our rate of water loss is a quart a day, the average person could lose that 10 percent in four days. If you dry out by cutting down your fluid intake or if you take diuretics and drain out, you're just causing a fluid imbalance. Poor health may result. Just as exercise may be governed, so must your rate of weight loss. Diuretics, which induce urination, are ineffective. You may lose a dramatic amount of weight rapidly. But this loss of essential body water is quickly regained.

Bulking agents, which swell in the stomach to create an undigested mass, give a feeling of fullness so the dieter eats less. Too high a dose, however, poses a danger of obstructing the intestine.

Appetite-suppressing drugs like amphetamines should be used extremely sparingly, if at all, because of their addictive characteristics and other side effects.

Actually, if there were an ideal diet drug, it would be one which increased energy expenditure by increasing heat production.

The body metabolizes through heat. It converts food into the structure of our body by changing that food into energy or heat. This energy is used in three ways: First, the body is continually dismantling and rebuilding itself. For example, the body replaces half its bone in six months, half its liver in ten days. Other energy is used for immediate and constant life-functioning processes: breathing, sleeping, eating, digestion. The remaining energy is stored, first as carbohydrates and then, fat.

Calories, as you probably know them, are measuring devices for weight loss. Actually, a calorie is a measure of heat. The amount of heat required to raise the temperature of one gram of water by one degree centigrade, to be exact. When you give off heat, you are expending energy created by the consumption of food or fat in your body.

One pound of flesh is equivalant to 3,500 calories. To lose a pound, you must burn off 3,500 more calories than you eat. You must create a deficit. The aim of all slimming diets is to reduce your energy intake below your energy expenditure. At the same time, however, it is important to maintain a nutritional balance, a metabolic balance, in order to maintain your health.

To lose that safe pound per week, you must have a calorie deficit of 500 calories per day. The average-sized adult eats about 2,400 calories a day. He uses about 2,300 per day. That 100 calorie difference is the cause of creeping obesity. Chances are you gained weight gradually. Lose it gradually, too.

To maintain a metabolic balance and still lose weight, you must eat a balanced diet and expend enough energy to create a daily deficit of 500 calories in order to lose a pound per week. Jumping rope in brief sessions three or four times per day expends about 500 calories.

Here you are, looking for a simple and efficient exercise and suddenly you are a mathematician. If you have a large weight problem (too much fat) consult your physician, get a rope, and become a mathematician who specializes in calorie counting.

If you have a flab problem, consult your physician, get a rope, and eat a variety of foods which give you a daily complement of the four basic food groups: meat, vegetables, grain and dairy products.

Preventive maintenance could be your motivation for experiencing my program. Welcome, elitist. You already realize that exercise can also play a very valuable role in stopping you from getting fat and flabby in the first place.

The right diet, combined with the right exercise, is a painless way to lose fat. You maintain your body's healthy balance, lose weight permanently, tone and trim your body, gain strength and energy, and feel better about the whole thing all at the same time!

Weight gain is often caused by certain changes in your life that occupy you so much that the added weight is there before you realize it. You may have started working at a job that involves a few too many business lunches and not enough time to exercise. Or, maybe you are a mother who stopped working to take care of your child and developed a habit of snacking at the playground. Maybe it's your first year in college and you are suddenly subjected to high calories in cafeteria and junk food.

Combining diet and exercise offers you a broader choice of how to lose that excess baggage. Of course, the extent of your fat-loss program depends upon whether that extra baggage is an overnight bag or a large suitcase. In other words, how much do you want to or have to lose? And what is your present state of fitness?

Say, for example, you have already become an expert in my jump-rope program. Can you eat all you want? That still depends upon how much overweight you are. Frankly, if you are on a regular, controlled cardiovascular exercise program, I doubt if you will feel the urge to *over*eat. I think you will become more aware of your body, what you are doing for and to it. Chances are you'll discover a distinction between eating all you want and overeating.

Eating the right foods is most important, *especially* if you are involved in a weight loss/fitness program. Before you decide to eliminate any foods essential to the balanced nutritional intake of your body, ask your doctor if it's okay.

How many calories should you eat per day, then? To maintain your weight, consume ten calories per day for each pound you weigh, if you get little physical activity. That means, if you are sedentary and are not doing anything about it, follow the above plan.

If you are joining us jumpers, eat fourteen calories per day per pound of weight to *maintain* your body weight.

If you are jumping and weigh 160, for example, consume 1,920 calories per day, or 13,440 per week. Since it takes 3,500 calories to produce a pound of fat, you can lose a pound a week by limiting yourself to 1,420 calories a day and following my jump-rope program.

Calorie expenditure varies with your weight. The energy cost for the average, quiet, sitting human is 72 calories per hour. In hard exercise, this amount may be increased by twentyfold or more. A person weighing 150 pounds will spend 210 calories per hour walking, 420 calories an hour playing tennis, 600 calories per hour skiing, 720 calories per hour running, and 760 calories jumping rope at 120–140 turns per minute for an hour.

You are not going to jump rope for an hour, so weight loss through exercise is going to take some time. That's good. The longer you take to lose it, the longer it will stay away.

A regular exercise program should cause you to burn calories in other ways, too. Your new philosophy about yourself should create a new energy within you so you move more than you used to. Instead of driving, you may decide to walk to the store and back. There went 210 calories you hadn't consciously thought about spending. You might decide to take the stairs at work every day instead of the elevator. You've got new energy now. You feel like moving. You didn't before. Maybe that's why the fat seem to just get fatter, while the thin stay thin. All you have to do is get moving, overcome inertia, and your body and mind will take it from there.

Jumping rope is a high-energy exercise. By its nature, it has a tremendous effect on body composition by causing it to burn the right fuel. Jumping is not so strenuous that it implies an emergency-energy situation to your body which ignites the carbohydrates, nor so taxing that it demands fuel from proteins. Jumping attacks good old fat. What a gold mine! The same exercise that enhances body composition (reduces fat) is also effective in the improvement of circulatory-respiratory endurance.

Remember, both your exercise and your diet must be programmed, paced, frequent, and regularly applied over a period of time. My program is designed so that you take the proper amount of time and pacing for maximum effectiveness. You must do the same with your diet plan. Remember, a pound a week and no more. Unless your doctor says differently.

One more point about weight loss. Often, especially if you are a woman, you have that particular trouble area where there is a load of fat and have heard about or tried what's referred to as "spot reducing." No sense putting on a whole new roof when there's only one hole by the chimney. Spot reducing doesn't really make the best of common sense.

First of all, as long as you are exercising, you might as well make the effort pay off in as many places as you can.

If you begin a specific exercise for a specific area, you are exercising specific muscles and ignoring the rest of you. You may wind up chasing that fat deposit *around* your body instead of getting it *off* your body.

Concentrating on particular muscles also may cause those muscles to build, to enlarge. So you trade the fat on your outer, upper thighs for much larger muscles. That won't shape you up. Jumping rope is a general shaping and toning exercise for as many parts of your body as possible. Given the opportunity, your body will rearrange itself to the best condition and shape it can possibly be.

Here are a few suggestions to help you lighten the load:

1. Set your caloric deficiency level.

2. Lose weight slowly, permanently.

3. If you can, avoid the "fright" foods like peanut butter, mayonnaise, French fries, and pie.

4. Keep your diet to yourself. If you fail, no one need know. Avoid the pressure of social success or failure.

5. If you slip up or let up in either your diet or exercise, don't go into a snit about it. Realize you are human. Just start again. Saints are sinners who keep trying.

6. Eat less and more often. There is evidence that food is used more efficiently when consumed in this manner.

7. Follow my jump-rope program as diligently as you can.

8. Cook for yourself as often as you can.

9. Consult your physician, especially if you are overweight.

10. Keep your jump rope in plain sight near the kitchen.

11. Make an appointment with a tailor or seamstress to take in your clothing to fit the new you!

X.
Who Can Jump?
(And When and Where?)

I can't emphasize enough the importance of consulting your physician prior to jumping. If you haven't had a physical in a while, make an appointment. Consider the encounter your first step in my jump-rope program. This is especially true if you are overweight, over 30, or have a history of cardiovascular illness.

If you are physically able, you can jump regardless of age.

CHILDREN AND ROPE SKIPPING

Children do not get enough exercise without conscious effort. That's hard to accept, particularly if you've ever tried following a toddler around for a while. Children seem to be unable to sit still. They want to move as much as they can, but they do not necessarily get the right kind of exercise or even sufficient real exercise. Improvements in fitness should begin as early as possible in life. Dr. Rodahl suggests that children be guided into a regular exercise program in addition to the exercise they may receive at play. What exercise does he suggest?

"As true for adults, few things are more effective in developing total fitness in a child than an ordinary skip rope. It will develop strength, coordination, and endurance, and it is fun. The children should be encouraged to carry their skip ropes with them to school and to the playground. They may spend the time skipping while waiting for the school bus if it is too far to walk to school. They may skip during recess. . . . Ordinary play engaged in by children following their own inclinations may not be of sufficient intensity and duration to have any training effect. What a person is able to do at the age of 70 depends largely on what he could do at seven."

"Hey, kids, you need an exercise program."

"Boooh, Hisss!"

"Yup, you're going to jump rope every day."

"Yeaaa!"

48

Now, you have an exercise vehicle that sounds like play. And it is. Guide the children into jumping at least once a day, five days a week. And set an example for them. Jump with them.

TEENAGERS AND ROPE SKIPPING

Jumping rope is great for the teenager. You may be growing one or two inches each year. Your coordination and agility may not be keeping up with that rapid growth pace. Jumping rope will help turn fatty tissue into lean muscle. Mildred Cooper in *Areobics for Women* cited a survey of 300 local high school students taken by the *Des Moines Register* which asked the kids if they thought they were getting enough exercise. Eighty-seven percent of the teenagers responded negatively. One student added: "I look at my mom and dad and see a very low level of fitness right now. They exercised a whole lot more when they were my age than I'm exercising. What am *I* going to look like when I'm their age?"

The onset of puberty begins a disproportionate growth in strength in boys over girls. Prior to puberty, boys and girls are equal in strength. Regular exercise offers a challenge to the teenage girl and reinforcement to the teenage boy.

YOUNG ADULTS AND ROPE SKIPPING

You are out of school now and into career, home, family, hobbies, friends. And it is not pleasant to think about the fact that cardiovascular disease accounts for 31 percent of all deaths of men and women between ages of 35 and 44. A study by William F. Enos and reported in the *Journal of the American Medical Association* in 1953 indicated that among 200 American servicemen with an average of 22.1 years who were killed in Korea, 77 percent already had some gross evidence of hardening of the arteries! At any age, jumping rope or any similar cardiovascular, aerobic exercise program is essential to insure fitness.

THE OLDER AND ROPE SKIPPING

The older you are, the more exercise you need. As a rule, as you grow older you have more time to exercise. That means you have no excuse to be inactive. Jumping develops endurance, reduces fatigue, stimulates metabolism, and improves aching joints and muscles. Exercise enhances your ability to move about and go places on your own and gives you the satisfaction of independence. Exercise, according to Dr. Rodahl, is the most important factor in the treatment of mild arthritis because it helps you to maintain joint function. But it has to be carried out under the supervision of a doctor. Dr. Rodahl even suggests that after two months of limbering and lesser exercises, persons over age 65 may begin a modified rope-jumping program with guidance from their physicians.

At the beginning and throughout any exercise, be aware of any clues which might indicate you are overworking your heart. Any pain you encounter while working out should be heeded. Stop jumping immediately, walk around, rest, and make an appointment with your physician.

Watch for pale or clammy skin, shakiness lasting more than ten minutes after jumping, leg cramps, nausea, blueing around the lips or fingernails, uneven heartbeats, pounding of the heart for more than five minutes after jumping, headache, or restlessness at night after the exercise.

Again, no matter what your age is, it's mandatory that you have medical supervision with your exercise program. If you are under 30 and have had a medical checkup within the past year, you can begin. If you are between 30 and 39, the medical checkup should have taken place within the past six months. If you are between 40 and 49, the exam should have been within the last three months and a resting ECG should have been included. If you are over 50, the medical checkup should be given immediately before starting my program and should include an ECG while exercising.

You are going to be more aware of your heart and lungs than you ever have been before. It may unnerve you at first, but if you have medical clearance, you can feel comfortable about using that new awareness to check your progress. Learn to take your pulse. After you jump, your rapid pulse beat will slow down. The further advanced you become in my program, the less time it will take for your pulse to slow down. If you are under 40, your pulse rate should drop to 120 beats per minute within three minutes after jumping. Ten minutes is too long. Check with your doctor.

My program is based on interval training designed to speed up your heart with short bursts of energy between rest periods. The speed at which your heart rate decelerates is a good measure of your progress.

Taking your pulse is easy. For a long time I was using my thumb, which provided me with the pulse rate in my thumb. That's not what you want. Place the first three fingers of your opposite hand lightly on your wrist about two inches from the base of the thumb and about an inch and a half from the end of your wrist.

Press your fingers into the groove between your wrist bone and the sinews next to it. Press gently and feel around. You'll find it. Count the beats for fifteen seconds and multiply by four. Nothing to it. Normal sitting heart rate is between 72 and 80 beats per minute. Anything below 50 and above 80 should inspire you to make an appointment with your physician.

Make certain your heartbeat does not exceed 130 beats per minute at the beginning stages of the program. Make sure you achieve your resting pulse rate within the tolerable time span discussed earlier.

Keeping track of your pulse can be quite a kick. Wait until you discover you have actually *lowered* your resting heart rate!

Correct method of taking your pulse

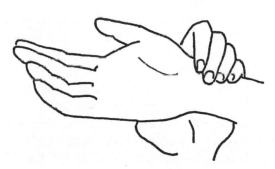

Place three fingers of your opposite hand lightly on your wrist, about two inches from the base of the thumb and about an inch and a half from the end of your wrist. Fingers should be placed in the groove between your wrist bone and the sinews next to it. Press gently and feel around. Count the beats for fifteen seconds and multiply by four.

Women and Jumping Rope

The female hormone, estrogen, is believed to be a built-in immunizing agent against coronary disease in women during their child-bearing years and may be a major factor in statistics which indicate more men die from heart attacks than women.

Physicians tried estrogen on men at one time. The trouble with the experiment was the men treated achieved protection at the expense of their masculinity, their beards, their voices, and their breasts, which became enlarged.

Estrogen is not a panacea against heart disease in women, especially today, when women are assuming more and more stressful occupations which used to be the private territory of men. Women today are faced with more stress than when their position in life was cast, by tradition, in the home. Despite the presence of estrogen, a woman needs regular exercise to protect her heart and arteries.

Exercise like my jump-rope program does not create bulging muscles and an unfeminine physique, as was once believed. Rope skipping shapes and tones, smooths and trims, rather than building large amounts of body mass. That's why I advised earlier against spot-reducing exercises. Wouldn't you rather go down a whole dress size than lose only an inch off the hips or thighs?

I've heard women say more than once, "Sure, the minute I start losing weight, do you know where I lose it first? Right here," accompanying the remark with a gesture toward the breasts. There is no guarantee you will increase, decrease, or retain the same bust size from jumping rope. I can guarantee, however, better support. First, you will firm up body tissue, including the tissue around your breasts.

Secondly, the motion of the arms and shoulders in rope jumping strengthens your pectoral muscles which support the breasts. So, whatever you have, you'll have better support of it. Or, them.

Exercise itself has no connection with tearing of connective tissues near the breasts. It is still important that you wear a supportive bra when jumping. This will protect the ligaments supporting the breasts and it will be downright more comfortable for you.

There was also a time when women who were experiencing their menstrual period couldn't do anything, let alone exercise. Today, most doctors agree that an exercise that improves circulation, muscular strength, and flexibility in the abdominal area can relieve cramps and lower backache, and the mental stress that goes along with it all. If you have a severe menstrual problem such as dysmenorrhea, ask your doctor about it.

Strenuous exercise during the first few months of pregnancy is strictly up to your physician, okay? Exercise prior to pregnancy is wise.

There is no question you want to have a strong body to carry that extra load and reduce the strain when you do become pregnant. After pregnancy, jumping rope will help you deflate, firm up, and trim up.

Menopausal women are faced with the loss of estrogen and the increasingly limited protection from heart disease. In its place should be employed the self-induced protectorate of cardiovascular exercise.

THE ACTIVE PERSON AND JUMPING ROPE

You may be a tradesperson or laborer or active in sports, and feel you are physically active enough to be at a desirable level of fitness. You could be right. Besides, after exercising for a living all day, who wants to work out more!

First, however, you must realize that there is a difference between physical activity and an exercise program. A program is balanced, progressive, and controlled to strengthen the life-sustaining functions of your body. That's why more and more professional atheletes who work out daily are jumping rope, too.

The fitter you are, the more it takes to improve your fitness. That, of course, is an advantage for you unfit folks. One of the few. In order to improve your level of fitness, you must do more than you do in your ordinary day, no matter what that is. The progression level is a key factor in evaluating exercise programs. It must advance in intensity, along with your advancing level of fitness. And whatever your activity level day-by-day, additional correct exercise reduces fatigue and stress.

Vigorous sports, like cross-country skiing and tennis, rival the intensity of rope skipping as a cardiovascular exercise. But participating in a sport, even regularly, is no guarantee of physical fitness, because the exercise is not controlled or paced.

THE UNCOORDINATED AND JUMPING ROPE

So far, the only restriction in my jump-rope program is medical. Only your doctor knows for sure.

For a time, I believed there were some people who were just plain too uncoordinated to get a rope under their feet without landing on it. Not that there was any physical problem. It was just one of those things they could not do. Like some people can't dance.

I don't believe that anymore. Anyone can jump rope. If you think you're clumsy, its probably because somebody said: "Hey, are you ever clumsy. You'll never do it." You'll do it. It may take you longer than others, but who's to know that? Jumping rope the right way, the professional way, is very impressive looking to outside observers. So here's your chance, former clumsy one, to break open that shell somebody put you in and come out skipping and dancing.

WHEN TO JUMP

There are night people and there are morning people. Some function best in the morning. Early risers hop out of bed full of energy and jubilance, greeting the rising sun with great zeal. About ten o'clock at night they disappear in a trail of yawns.

Night people don't understand why early risers act that way in the morning. Getting up and getting a head of steam takes time for them. Reaching peak performance usually doesn't happen for slow-risers until later in the day. For the morning people, fatigue at night is as natural as morning fatigue is for night people.

It's not certain why there are these kinds of differences between people. One theory suggests differences in basic biological rhythms. And it has been learned that a person's 24-hour biological rhythm is associated with a certain pattern in his metabolic processes. People tested by being kept in continuous darkness or light maintained their night or morning differences, which implied the differences are characteristic to the individual.

So should you jump during your best or worst part of the day? During the first three weeks of my program, you will be jumping more than once a day. I suggest you spread these periods throughout the day. If you are a morning person, jump right after you get out of bed, at noon, and in early evening.

If you are night owl, take your first exercise as soon as you are certain you are awake. Probably, noon. Repeat in the early evening, and again before retiring. Don't try to change what may be biological patterns. Make it easy on yourself. The answer to when-should-I-jump, then, is: Exercise when you are feeling your best.

Jumping rope is so convenient and quick you can do it just about anytime and anywhere. Although I suggest you jump during your peak hours, there are specific times when jumping can aid specific problems.

1. As mentioned earlier, jump to the special exercises in "Jumping for Sports" just prior to an athletic event or recreation.

2. If you are on a fat-loss program, jump just prior to breakfast, lunch or late-night snacktime. Exercise, especially cardiovascular activity, has a tendency to curb your appetite.

3. Paradoxically, jumping rope can relax you when you are over-

stimulated and provide you energy when you are fatigued. So you may have to figure out for yourself whether jumping just before bedtime puts you to sleep or makes you feel wide awake. Your fatigue may be caused by emotional stress. Jumping will discharge tension, soak up excess nervous energy, and help you get your mind off the sore spot.

In summary, jump when you are hungry, when you are fatigued, when you are angry, when you are frustrated, when you want to drink or smoke, whenever you face physical, mental or emotional stress.

WHEN *NOT* TO JUMP

Don't jump every day. My program calls for a five-out-of-seven day week of exercising. How you want to select the days is up to you, but be sure to take a couple of days off.

Don't jump when you don't feel well. Don't punish yourself. Promise me that. Top athletes, as we have said, may excel in tremendously taxing sports events while suffering from the flu or other ailments in the same way you go to work and push on in spite of how crummy you may feel. But to the athelete, that contest is his job. He's trained for it, as you are for your work. Athletes can summon the extra effort without complications to their body. You can't, and shouldn't, with the present shape your body is in. If you've got a bug, just take care of yourself.

Don't jump if you are not cognizant of your current state of fitness. In other words . . . all together now . . . "A MEDICAL EXAM." Right!

Don't jump until you warm up. We'll talk about the value and methods of limbering up before vigorous exercise in the chapter, "Firing Up."

Earlier, I mentioned how sometimes late at night, I'll get up and jump if I'm feeling restless or tense. Don't jump when other people are sleeping until you are ready for noiseless jumping. The wife of a business associate told me she quit jumping for a time because of the noise it made. "We lived in an apartment then," she explained, "and my jumping prompted the neighbors to pound on the ceiling below, both in imitation of the sounds I was making and in protest." She now jumps noiselessly. The difference between noisy and noiseless jumping is what you are soon to learn. And it is part of what makes jumping rope easy, fun, effective, and quiet.

I've seen joggers puffing alone, in weather I didn't even care to drive in. If it's a hot, humid day, relax and wait until tomorrow. If you live or work in a room so small you have to go outside to change your mind, let alone jump, don't jump out-of-doors in severe weather . . . extremely cold, hot, humid, or other types of severe inclemency.

WHERE TO JUMP

Once you have become a jumper . . . when you have mastered the surprisingly simple method of control I am going to teach you, you may jump in an area as small as a walk-in closet. You can jump in a hallway at home or at work, in the living room, basement, sidewalk, street, kitchen, bedroom, or garage. Your rope needs to clear an area three feet over your head, eight inches on each side of you, and four feet in front and back of you. Picture a box 8 feet long, 9½ feet high, and 4 feet wide. That's just about the most area you will need to work in.

XI.
On the Ropes

You can spend as little as a handful of pennies or as much as ten dollars on a jump rope. You get what you pay for. A piece of clothesline or a sash cord will do. It may be cotton, nylon, or polyethylene. You can even jump with a length of surgical tubing if you wish. I've heard of a weightlifter who used a 45 pound chain!

If you jumped for play as a child, jumping rope will come easier to you. After a shaky start, it will be just like old times. If you've never jumped, you may find twirling a rope a bit more awkward in the beginning. I don't want you to become discouraged because you find jumping rope not so easy, at first, as I led you to believe.

That's why I recommend a balanced and weighted rope for beginners. You'll find these custom ropes on the market in a variety of styles. The weight and balance allows you to turn the rope more easily and fluidly. Handles on these ropes are usually made of wood or plastic and are shaped for a surer grip.

Soon, you will learn how to turn the rope with just your hands and wrists while your arms remain nearly stationary. Commercial ropes are made so the rope passes through the handles and is knotted on the ends. This facilitates a free-turning rope while the handles remain stationary.

A more deluxe feature in some ropes is the ball-bearing handle, which provides greater speed as you progress in the program. If going first class offers you inspiration, you'll find a leather rope, balanced and weighted with ball-bearing handle action, on the market.

All you really need is a clothesline to begin the jump-rope program. Remember, though, you are no longer jumping to *pass* the time . . you are jumping to *preserve* time. The time of your life. So make it easy on yourself. Select a rope which fits your needs.

If you make your own rope, the cord should be about 3/8 of an inch thick and about 8½ feet long, depending upon your height. The lighter the rope, the thicker it should be. A good weight for your needs is ordinary sash cord, which is available at almost any hardware store. Tie the ends of the rope in a knot to prevent fraying. Make sure the rope is the right length for you. The rope should not slap on the floor when you jump. If it does, it is too long.

Set the rope length by standing on the center of the rope with one foot. The two ends or handles should reach your armpits.

Once you start jumping, you may want to make minor adjustments in the length of your rope. Some advanced jumpers prefer their ropes longer to allow for more dexterity and maneuverability in performing more intricate skips and stunts.

You may find it valuable to have more than one rope. Keep one at home and one at the office. A friend hangs his rope inside his garage. When he comes home, he jumps for a few minutes before he goes in for supper.

You'll get to know your rope pretty well. My wife Jannelle and I get ours mixed up sometimes. More than once I've picked up a rope to jump only to have it suddenly wrap around my ankles two inches shorter than it should be. "Funny," grins Janelle, "mine is too long all of a sudden." Reminds me of Laurel and Hardy exchanging hats.

Now that you have your rope, you may be tempted to take a few jumps. Go ahead. Just a few. Then stop. Jumping rope is not a painful or difficult exercise, but it is a strenuous one. You have to warm up to it. You must fire up.

Aha! Thought you caught me, huh? Thought I would miss a chapter in reminding you to get a physical checkup before embarking on my jump rope or any exercise program. Of course, wise and sensible person that you are, you've already made an appointment, haven't you?

Adjusting your rope

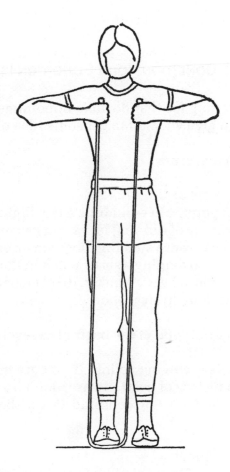

Set the rope length by standing on the center of the rope with one foot. The two ends or handles should reach your armpits.

XII.
Firing Up

Finding Out the Condition Your Condition Is In

While you are waiting for that doctor's appointment, there are some simple tests you can give yourself to get some idea of your present state of fitness.

The first test is an oral exam.

Test I: Ask yourself these questions:
1. Does your heart pound after climbing a few flights of stairs?
2. Does a short distance of running leave you gasping for air?
3. Is tieing a shoelace from a standing position an effort for you?
4. Do you get sore from digging a small patch in the garden?
5. Are you overweight, a heavy smoker, drinker, or all three?
6. Do you tend to avoid physical effort if you can?

One "Yes" answer puts you at the beginning level of physical fitness. (Join the Crowd.)

Now for some tests involving action. If you are undergoing medical treatment or have a history of heart disease, don't try these tests without a doctor's advice. And do not continue if you begin to feel overly stressed.

Test II: Physical measures
1. Take a deep breath. Can you hold it for at least forty-five seconds?
2. Let all the air out of your lungs and measure your chest. Then inhale as much as you can and remeasure. The difference should be at least 3½ inches for men and 2½ inches for women.
3. Step up and down on a chair which is somewhere near 15 inches off the floor. Alternate your steps. Can you do this 20 times?
4. Run in place for 3 minutes. Then, take your pulse. Is it under 120 beats a minute?

If you failed any of these tests, you are still at the beginning level of fitness. This next series of tests examines your pulse rate, so make sure that you allow at least five minutes between each test.

TEST III: MORE PHYSICAL MEASURES

1. Hop up and down 20 times. Remain standing for one minute after hopping. Then count your pulse for 15 seconds. Did you have 17 beats or under?

2. Climb 10 steps of a flight of stairs without a stop, starting at the foot of the stairs and climbing and descending and climbing again as fast as you can. Take your pulse for 15 seconds immediately after the exercise. Did you complete the chore in 15 seconds or less and was your pulse rate 30 or under?

3. Test your legs by consecutive deep knee bends without support. Start standing with your hands stretched out in front of you. Bend down as far as you can, keeping your back straight. Let your arms drop and fingers touch the floor. Were you able to do this at least 25 consecutive times?

4. Lay on the floor with your hands at your sides. Get up to a standing position, turn around once completely and lie back down again into the starting position. Did you complete this coordination test in less than 5 seconds?

5. Sit on a chair at a table and put both hands on the table, palms down. Start tapping the table with your right hand at a rate of about 2 taps per second. At the same time, slowly run your left hand along the table's edge from right to left for a distance of about one foot, without interrupting in any way the tapping rate of the right hand. Were you able to do it in 3 tries?

6. Set the faucet in the kitchen or bathroom sink so it drips at the rate of about one drop every second. Now, place your hand palm up 3 inches away from the water's path and 3 inches below the faucet. Watch the drop appear below the faucet and try to catch it on your hand by moving your hand horizontally. Were you able to do it in 3 tries?

7. Stand up, put your heels together, raise your arms forward to shoulder level, lift both heels off the floor. When you have balance, close your eyes and see how long you can stay in this position. Were you able to sustain for 10 seconds or longer?

8. Undress. Stand in the middle of the floor and, without support, dress yourself completely without having to sit down or hold on to anything. Did you succeed?

How did you do? If you failed any of these simple tests, you are at the beginning fitness level and you need a week of exercising preparatory to jumping rope. If you are over fifty, I suggest you use these first week exercises no matter how well you did on the fitness test. These exercises will limber you, strengthen your muscles and prepare you to receive graciously the real exercise to come. The following preliminary workouts are not glamorous or fun like jumping rope. Just keep in mind that they are essential and it's only for a few days.

GETTING IN SHAPE TO JUMP

Each day for five days, do the following:

KNEE BENDS

As in the fitness test, stand with your feet about 6 inches apart, your arms raised forward to shoulder height. Lift up on your toes, then bend your knees slowly as far as you can while dropping your arms simultaneously until your fingers touch the floor. Hold for 3 seconds, rise, and bring your arms back up to shoulder height. Do 5 the first day and add 3 per day. Note: Do not attempt that old exercise of touching the floor with your hands while your legs are straight and stiff. Any time you bend over, your knees should bend, too. It's easier and healthier for your back.

BOXING, KICKING, AND SCRATCHING

Men are familiar with the first part of this exercise. It is like the professional fighter's warm-up before the big bout. Women, try this too. Bend forward slightly in a crouch and start making imaginary roundhouse punches in the air. Swing your arms wide at an imaginary target as your feet shuffle and dance toward and away from the target. Do this vigorously for about 30 seconds, then switch to the kick. This movement is probably more familiar to women, but men should do it, too. Put your arms up at your sides as if they were around imaginary members of your chorus line. Alternately, bring your leg up with a knee bend. Then kick each leg out in front of you as high as you can without strain. Do this for 30 seconds. Now, get on your hands and knees. Start clawing the air with your hands and arms like a cat in a fight. Raise up on your knees and claw with both hands at an imaginary foe. Go ahead and hiss and spit if you want to. I know this sounds silly. It also looks silly. But it will help stretch and limber those muscles. Do it for 30 seconds. Double this exercise each day.

Imaginary Swimming

Stand with your feet wide apart and let your trunk fall forward to a point where you are bent over but relaxed. Do the crawl stroke, alternating each arm. Feel the force of the imaginary body of water against your open palms. Pull against it. Lift up your head and breathe as you would while swimming. Do this for 20 strokes. Add 5 strokes a day.

Running-in-Place

It is important to move your arms as if you were running a distance in this exercise. Let them swing vigorously. The action helps your diaphragm move and your circulation build. Lift your knees as high as you can. Take 50 steps the first day. Add 30 steps each day for 5 days.

Hopping

Hop up and down on both feet. This time, keep your arms down and about 8 inches out from your body. Turn your closed fists outward. (Like you had a jump rope in your hand. Hang on. Hang on. Soon, you will). As you hop, bend your body forward slightly, knees bent and land on the balls of your feet. While hopping, try making little circling motions with your fists. Hop 25 times the first day and add 10 hops per day for 5 days.

The Jelly Roll

Stand and let your arms hang loosely by your sides. Lift and rotate your shoulders in a circular motion upward, forward, downward, and backward. Make 20 circles, changing direction every 5 times. Finally, let the roll extend down your trunk to the waist and hips until you feel your torso rolling on the base of your hips and legs. Do this for about 10 turns. Try to roll in each direction as far as you can, without tipping over.

These exercises will help you limber up in preparation for your jump-rope program. They will stretch and soften those tight muscles. Do not exercise beyond my recommendations, especially if you are at the beginning fitness level, over 50, or overweight. Exertion which becomes too much of a surprise to your body may cause your body to have a surprise for you the next morning. Any stiffness or soreness you might experience will be too reminiscent of the old pain myth we dispensed with earlier. And you can get that kind of grief without this workbook.

I have two more exercises for you that you can use not only in your warm-up week, but throughout my program and the rest of your life. Be aware of your body while you are at your daily routine. Make a conscious effort, if you have been sitting for a long time, to stop, let your shoulders droop, close your eyes, and roll your head backward, to one side, forward, and to the other side in a circular motion. Stretch the muscles and relax for a minute.

Stand up and do your favorite stretching movements. My grand stretch, my really big one, consists of standing on my toes with my chest out, head back and my arms making a huge, slow circular motion like a high-board diver doing a swan dive. This stretch is usually accompanied by a loud, "Gggghhaaaahhhhh!" sound.

Finally, here is a natural exercise that's fun to do. It's also good for you. It exercises the diaphragm and circulatory system and helps expand those chest muscles. It's called: laughter. One of the best fitness exercises you can find. Apply it more often.

What to Wear While Exercising

Wear light, loose-fitting porous clothing. Do not wear thick or nonporous material like rubberized sweatsuits or windbreaker type clothing. It's important to let your skin breath as your body heats up. Men should wear a jockstrap or firm cotton Jockey shorts for proper support against the vigorous up-and-down motion your body is going to make. Similarly, women should wear a bra to support the breasts against this movement. Wear something that supports you firmly, but avoid bras that are too tight. Do not wear girdles, corsets, or garters.

Wear a pair of absorbent socks. If you can, wear some sort of soft, heelless shoe such as tennis shoes. You will find jumping rope easier if you wear a shoe that is light, porous, and gives you a spring in your step. As you advance, you'll want to take advantage of the convenience and portability of jumping rope. That means, if you are at the office and wearing oxfords, jump in your oxfords. If you are wearing flats, that's fine. I wouldn't recommend jumping in heels unless you are expert. It is a good idea to keep a pair of "jumping" shoes at work.

Whatever you do, don't jump in stocking or bare feet. Shoes give your feet support as you land up and down on the balls of your feet. And you'll also avoid sore toes. I learned the hard way. One morning I jumped in my stocking feet in the bedroom. I had a commercial rope which was weighted by dozens of plastic extrusions or sleeves around the rope. I liked the lack of weight on my feet, so I thought I'd just jump shoeless. I was going at a pretty good clip and proud of it, when suddenly the rope caught right on the end of both sets of toes! It was the first

64

time jumping rope helped me exercise my larynx. I yelled. It smarts. Don't jump without some sort of protective footwear. Save your toes.

JUMPING AND TWIRLING

It's time to learn to jump and twirl. We're ready if you are. If you are in the beginning level of fitness and have completed your week of preparatory exercises, you are ready and no doubt anxious, too. If you are not certain, go back and take another shot at the fitness tests we gave you earlier. Make sure you pass each test. If you don't, take another few days of prep.

Rope skipping demands hand-mind-feet coordination. So much so that you must practice the various movements separately. *Jump without the rope.* Your hands and feet must practice their individual assignments first if they are to work together later.

My program calls for a week of this training before you actually jump rope. I am not so much concerned yet about the pacing of the program as I am about your development of coordination among your hands, mind and feet. If you feel you are not ready at the end of one week, take a second week and practice the exercises that follow again until you feel comfortable and confident.

You are continuing to condition your body as you learn the jumps. Therefore I have established maximums which you should not exceed during the Jump and Twirl training session. We will check your pulse regularly during these preparatory exercises, so be sure to have a watch or clock with a sweep second hand nearby.

You are now officially in training. And from now on and as long as you continue to jump, you will never be the same. You will be more than you ever thought you could be.

Here we go:

THE TWO-FOOTED JUMP

Remember: NO ROPE YET. This is where your mind and your feet get to know each other. Jumping up and down on two feet is very easy. You've done it all your life. Right now, we want to establish your form. Stand in front of a mirror. Place your feet together, legs relaxed but steady and slightly bent at the knees. Keep your elbows and forearms relaxed at your sides. Now, raise your hands so they are about 5 inches in front of your waist, palms and fingers extended. (Imagine you're holding a bucket of water in each hand.) Close your hands and make fists. Look at yourself in the mirror.

Feet together. Knees slightly bent, elbows and forearms close at your sides. Hands facing upward and outward and about 5 inches away from your waist. Fists closed. Turn sideways. Your body should be bent forward at the waist slightly. As you jump, this leaning forward position is a natural one and you should yield to it. It is physically protective of your calf muscles and the tendons around your ankles. If you have heard that some dancers get big calves, it's probably because they do not utilize this natural forward bend in their practices.

This is your stance. Study it and then look away from the mirror so it doesn't confuse you. From now on when you jump, look straight ahead. Do not look at your feet. Straight ahead.

Start jumping up and down, slowly, pushing off with your toes and landing on the balls of your feet. Be sure you aren't jumping more than one inch off the floor. Jump at a rate between 60 and 70 jumps per minute. Do not jump for more than one minute without resting for five minutes.

Practice this initial step until you feel comfortable, but take it easy. Don't overdo it. If your heart pounds or you get out of breath, rest.

That's enough for your first day.

THE ONE-TWO JUMP

Today, the second day of your Jump and Twirl training, let's try the second of the basic jump steps you will be using. Most people find it convenient to start jumping with both feet together, using the Two-Footed Jump, but it is more effective as a training method to jump from foot-to-foot as if you were running in place. The One-Two Jump is a starting place.

You are still jumping without a rope.

Get in your ready position. Feet together, legs relaxed, elbows and forearms relaxed but close to your sides, fists turned outward. Push off with your toes and land on the balls of your feet. Look straight ahead. Using 2 jumps per foot, alternate your jump . . . first with one foot, counting "one-two," then the other, counting "one-two." Remember hopscotch? To get the right feel, jump with both feet together 3 or 4 times and then move into the alternating One-Two Jump. Make certain your foot is raised in front of your body (as if you were marching) instead of behind you. When you get to the rope, you might catch your foot on it if you step too far backward.

Jump at between 60 and 70 jumps per minute, but do not exceed one minute of jumping without resting. Work on the Two-footed and One-Two jumps until you are comfortable with them. After one minute of practice, rest for 5 minutes. Then, do 50 Two-Footed Jumps followed by 25 One-Two Jumps.

Jumping is a natural movement and you might feel like twirling your fists and wrists. Try it and match the rhythm of your jumping with the turning of your wrists. That's it for today. Stop. Remain standing. Walk around. Take your pulse. Make sure it is within the prescribed limits for you.

THE JOGGING JUMP

Today, your third day in training, you'll learn the third basic jumping step . . . a natural progression from the two previous steps. The Jogging Jump is similar to a normal jogging-in-place exercise except that you *jump* from foot to foot. Start with the Two-Footed Jump. Remember you are still not not using the rope.

Jump, lifting off from your toes and landing on the ball of your foot, knees slightly bent, arms at your side with fists turned outward while you are looking straight ahead.

Jump two-footed a few times and enter the One-Two Jump. After a few One-Two Jumps, eliminate the "two" part of the jump and hop only one jump on each foot. Lift your foot in front of your body. Don't kick your heels behind you as if you were running. Concentrate on keeping your foot in front of you, as if you were marching in place.

Practice the Jogging Jump for no longer than one minute. Rest for five minutes. Now, do 20 Two-Footed Jumps, followed by 20 One-Two Jumps and finish with 50 Jogging Jumps. Stop. Walk around for 30 seconds before you sit down. Take your pulse. It should not exceed 120 to 130 beats per minute. That's enough for today.

But take heart. Tomorrow is *Rope Day!*

THE TWIRLING MOVEMENT

Today is your fourth day of training and a special day. You get to use your rope. We're going to get your arms, wrists, and hands going, now. Stand in a stationary position and begin the twirling motions of your arms and wrists. Your elbows should be fairly close to your body and your arms extended out.

Okay. Now hold both handles of the jump rope in one hand. It doesn't matter whether it is your right or left. Use whichever is more comfortable. The twirling training itself is not vigorous, so work at your own pace. We are in no hurry. Keep in mind that the twirling rope is essentially arm and wrist action, while the up-and-down jumping helps activate this arm and wrist motion.

Without jumping, start twirling the rope in a circular motion at your side. Make sure you aren't near any chandeliers or delicate lamps. Eventually, you will be able to jump and twirl in a surprisingly small area. As soon as you learn control, that is. My first spin of the rope was stopped abruptly by a door knob behind me. Next, I nicked the ceiling fixture above me. Paranoia set in and I held back the loop as it passed over my head . . . with enought hesitation to bring the rope down from midflight to coil around my neck. I stopped right there and got to know my rope *before* jumping over it. I want you to get the feel of the twirling rope. Listen to it whirr. Let it touch the floor slightly.

As you turn your rope at your side, reach over and place your free hand on the rope handles so that both arms are swinging it. Hold your arms close to your waist, with your forearms parallel to the floor. Concentrate on using only your wrists and hands to turn the rope.

As you turn the rope with both hands on one or the other side of you, bring the spinning rope in front of you like a propeller on an airplane. You'll need more room for this exercise.

Notice that the smaller the rotation of your wrists and arms, the faster the rotation of the rope.

Spend three or four minutes twirling the rope while standing stationary. Twirl it on both sides and in front of you, and then relax for a few minutes.

Start twirling the rope at the side of you, using both hands. Look straight ahead and listen to the rhythm of the rope as it brushes the floor. After about ten twirls with the rope spinning at your side, begin jumping in rhythm to it. Push off with your toes not more than an inch off the floor and land on the balls of your feet. You are not jumping over the rope. It is turning at your side. Use the Two-Footed Jump and try to hop each time the rope touches the floor. Practice this until your hops are timed exactly with the rope sounds. Don't look at the rope. Listen to it. Stop hopping after 50 hops.

Rest two minutes. Now start the twirling action of the rope at your side again and begin with the Two-Footed Jump. After ten jumps, change to the One-Two Jump in rhythm to the rope. Do 25 One-Two jumps and change to the Jogging Jump. Do 30 Jogging Jumps and call it a day. Walk around and take your pulse. It shouldn't be over 125. If it is and you have had a medical exam within three months, contact your physician. If you haven't had an exam, do nothing more until you do.

Today is your fifth day of Jump and Twirl training. Your last day to coordinate your hands, mind and feet to work together in rope skipping. Start twirling the rope as before, holding the two handles together with both hands and twirling the rope on either your left or right side. After about ten twirls, start the Two-Footed Jump. Do 25 and then switch to the One-Two Jump and do 25 jumps. Switch without stopping into the Jogging Jump for 30 jumps. Stop. Walk around. Check your pulse. It should not exceed 125 beats per minute.

If you feel accomplished enough, you can vary the twirling exercise by moving the swinging rope in front of you and then to your other side while jumping in time to it. Change from two-handed twirling to one hand and switch it from your right to left hand and back again while jumping in sequence.

The above time limits are to protect you from over-exertion until your body is ready. If you feel you haven't mastered the rope and step combinations, add another day of these exercises. Give yourself some time. Don't expect mastery in minutes. Keep at it until you feel your hands and feet working together.

The Twirling Movement

As the rope is twirling at your side, jump by pushing off with your toes and landing on the balls of your feet.

Proper Jumping Form

Start with the rope at your heels behind you. Feet together, legs relaxed and steady, looking straight ahead. Push off with your toes and land on the balls of your feet. Keep your arm movement at a minimum, using your wrists and forearms to turn the rope. Your jump should only be high enough for the rope to clear. About one inch maximum.

The Two-Footed Jump

Keep your feet together, legs relaxed but steady, pushing off with your toes and landing on the balls of your feet. Your feet should not go higher than one inch off the floor.

The One-Two Jump

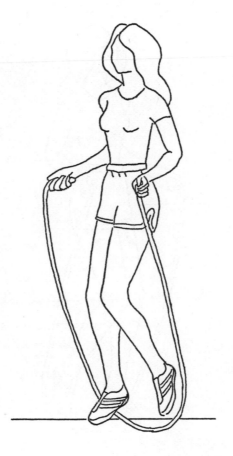

Using two jumps per foot, jump alternately counting "one-two" on each foot. Make sure you raise your feet in front of your body.

The Jogging Jump

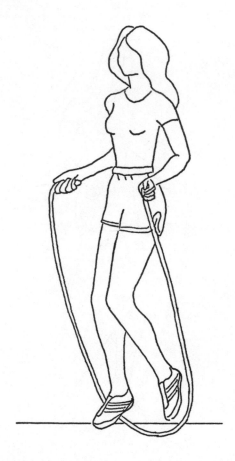

This jump is like the One-Two Jump except you jump only one count per foot. Jump from foot to foot, as if jogging in place. Try to keep your kickback at a minimum to avoid tangling with the rope.

XIII.
The Greg Campbell Jump-Rope Exercise Program

How long have you been practicing jumping and twirling separately? A week? Ten Days? Two weeks? The time it has taken you to become accustomed to the movements is arbitrary but necessary. Soon you will be on a regular, paced, and progressive jumping program. I want to make certain the rope feels comfortable to you. If this coordination bout has been difficult, don't worry about it. It will become easy. It's important for you to warm up and cool down before and after participating in a vigorous cardiovascular exercise.

Before each session, limber up and warm up by combining the knee bend, swimming, and kicking exercises you learned in the fitness test. Spend at least a full minute warming up with these exercises. Follow this series by standing erect and rolling your shoulders forward and backward to loosen up more muscles.

After you exercise, do not flop on the couch or in a chair. Walk around. Stay on your feet for at least two minutes after working out.

You know, a strange thing is soon to take place. Something will eventually happen to you not long after you master the rope. It's difficult to describe. It's a flow, a buzz, a hum, a high, a glow, a force that permeates you.

One day, you'll be struggling with your rope as before and it will happen. The whirr of the loop overhead becomes part of your body in motion, the beat of the rope becomes your heart, and you can feel the strength growing, coursing through you. You barely feel your feet touch the floor. You fly. Really. It's worth working for.

By now, you should have been medically cleared to begin this program, especially if you are over thirty or overweight.

Remember, too, that limbering up exercises prior to jumping are important. They allow the blood vessels in the muscles to dilate, which lets the blood rush unencumbered through the muscles in preparation for the greater effort that is to follow. It prevents the blood pressure from rising too high or too abruptly.

My program is designed to fit your age and fitness level. There are special programs also for the sports enthusiast (See Chapter XIV, Jumping for Sports), the overweight, and the older person. Your program must be carefully paced to increase with both intensity and duration to achieve cardiovascular efficiency. And the fitter you are initially, the more it takes to improve your fitness. That's why an unfit person will achieve amazing improvement in a surprisingly short time.

The following programs may be followed as a general guide if you do not fall into special groups such as advanced age, more than fifteen pounds overweight, or are under medical supervision.

YOUR FIRST WEEK

If you qualify, this next week is devoted to getting to know the three basic jumping steps *with* the rope. There are three to four sessions each of the five exercise days. Utilize a different step during each of the sessions and concentrate on it. Later, you will be able to change from one step to another without stopping.

I prefer you have four sessions per day the first week if you are up to it. "Up to it" means you are not over-exerting yourself. Over-exertion can be checked by taking your pulse. Your exercising heart rate should not exceed:

133 if you are 30 or under	119 if you are between 40 and 50
126 if you are between 30 and 40	112 if you are between 50 and 60.

These figures represent 70 percent of your maximum heart rate as compared to the average maximum for your particular age category. Physiologists recommend this control procedure in developing greater cardiovascular efficiency: raising your heart rate to 70 percent of your maximum for a short but sustained period of time. The guide above represents normal heart rates. Jumping rope will make your heart pound and will cause you to breathe heavily. That's normal. However, sedentary people who experience muscular, circulatory, or respiratory distress in reaching and maintaining their 70 percent of maximum heart rate should not press to achieve the average rate in the chart, but should gradually build up to the point where this level can be reached without undue discomfort.

If you are beyond the beginning fitness level, you should be able to achieve the 70 percent of maximum fairly easily and may go on to continue to a higher rate. We are out to adjust two heart rates: We want to gradually *increase* maximum heart rate so that you are able to sustain an *exercising rate* of between 130 and 150 beats per minute, depending upon your age; and we want to *lower* your *resting heart rate* below 70 beats per minute.

JUMPING OVER THE ROPE

Stand erect, looking straight ahead, and hold one handle of the rope in each hand. The loop of the rope should be resting on the floor behind you at your heels. Extend your arms forward for the initial swing. Rather than swing the rope once it gets going, rotate it with your wrists, hands and lower arms. Jump high enough for the rope to clear. No higher. Lift off and land on the balls of your feet. If the rope slaps on the floor, it is too long. If you are having trouble clearing the rope when you jump, it is too short.

Begin your first session with the Two-Footed Jump. Use the One-Two Jump the next session. The third session, jump the Jogging Jump, and so on. Remember when you jump, don't look at your feet. Look straight ahead. Stay relaxed and land on the balls of your feet. Jumping rope demands coordination, but it comes gradually so don't be discouraged. Almost everyone can manage to master it eventually. Even those people who are especially clumsy have learned.

THE TANGLES

Don't get upset when the rope tangles. If it tangles at your back, speed up the turns to maintain your loop. It is difficult to maintain a loop at a speed under 60 turns a minute. Tighten up the turn of your wrists and arms and keep your elbows in. When the rope tangles, stop and take a deep breath in and out. Then nonchalantly remove your feet and legs from the tangle, place the loop by your heels, and re-start calmly. Don't worry about it. You are going to tangle even if you are an accomplished rope jumper . . . even if you were the best kid on your block years ago.

When you jumped in those days, you probably started jumping higher or speeding or slowing the rope to compensate when you felt yourself slipping out of sequence. You tried to avoid tangling. I don't allow any margin for that in my rope-skipping style. I would rather you tangled than jump too high off the ground or not maintain the prescribed number of revolutions per minute. So, expect it. You are going to tangle. In fact, I think you must tangle in order to learn the right way to jump rope.

When you do tangle, don't start over. Resume where you left off in your count. Restart calmly, but as quickly as you can. This is especially important as you progress. Part of the success in achieving cardiovascular energy results from working your system at a specified pace for a prescribed period of time. If you wait too long between jumps to brood about your tangling, you will negate the effects we are trying to achieve.

During your first week in the program, master the three basic steps with the rope. We'll begin combinations next week.

HOW FAST AM I GOING?

You are the timekeeper in this program unless you have a willing friend or mate nearby who will keep track of things for you. Otherwise, jump near a clock. You can use the oven timer on the stove. You might feel a tendency to speed up once you are proficient in jumping. I would rather you didn't go faster than the prescribed amounts. Count your jumps and watch the clock. Eventually you'll get to know your pace and come within a few turns of it. You might consider purchasing a small metronome to really set your pace correctly.

Don't overdo it. Jumping is strenuous on your heart and lungs. Over-exercising can also put a strain on your muscles. I wouldn't want you discouraged by tenderness or soreness, especially when it definitely is not necessary.

LEARNING NEW STEPS

During the remainder of the program you should be able to combine the three basic steps as well as some intermediate steps found ahead in the book.

As you learn a new step, you will need to slow your pace possibly back to where you were a couple of weeks prior.

Wait until you are in your seventh week of jumping, if you are a woman, and your sixth week of jumping, if you are a man, before you try any intermediate steps. Delay trying the advanced steps until your twelfth week of my program.

Jump at least five minutes at your time and speed level before entering any period of intermittent jumping to learn new steps. This measure will maintain your level of fitness improvement.

SPECIAL PROGRAM FOR THOSE OVER 60

If you are over 60 years of age and have medical approval, follow this special program: After you have limbered up with the special warm-up exercises, skip on a soft surface such as your carpet or the the lawn. Skip with both feet together to start. Later you may change to the Jogging and One-Two Jumps. Start with only 10 skips the first day. Jump at 60 to 70 turns per minute. Each day, add 5 skips until you reach that day when you can do 100 consecutive skips. (Resume counting from where you left off after a tangle) Do 100 skips per day from then on. Speak with your doctor about whether or not you can increase your pace and duration.

SPECIAL PROGRAM IF YOU ARE OVERWEIGHT.

If you are fifteen pounds or more overweight, begin your first day of jumping with the Two-footed Jump at 60 to 70 turns per minute. Jump only 50 times the first day. Add 5 jumps a day to the 50 until you can do 70 jumps consecutively by the end of the first week.

Start the second week with the One-Two Jump at 60 steps. Try to complete the 60 steps in one minute. Come as close as you can to the sixty seconds. Add 10 steps a day at the 60 to 70 jumps per minute pace, until by the end of the second week you are able to jump 100 consecutive jumps. Begin my standard program at the first-week level at the start of your third week of jumping.

How Are You Feeling?

After your session, can you feel your heart pounding? Are you gasping for breath? Plan on it. You are training your body to consume more oxygen. You are getting fit. Make certian you master the three basic steps, because they form the foundation of a number of variations as you become more advanced. And the variations are limitless. I told you you wouldn't be bored. Once you have accomplished the first half of the program, you may try some new steps. There are dozens of them. By the time you have mastered all of mine, you'll be ready to invent your own. There is always something to look forward to in fitness.

Remember, your improvement may be more subtle in some ways than you thought. My neighbor tells of how he was jumping along in his third week, not really thinking about signs of improvement at the moment. He was too elated at the fact that he had mastered the correct art of jumping at all. "I was jumping in the bedroom and my wife started talking to me from the hallway. I was talking back to her for a good 30 seconds when I realized I was carrying on what felt like a normal conversation while jumping rope! I wan't gasping out words. I was just talking. There was no effort. I knew then I had come a long way already." What had left him huffing and puffing three weeks earlier was gone. His capacity to take in oxygen had already increased to a point where he needed much more energy output to cause him to be out of breath. At this point, what does it take to get *you* out of breath?

On Specific Programs

In addition to the special programs for the sports enthusiast, the older aged, the overweight and men and women, you'll find tailored programs for those who want to concentrate on specific parts of their bodies. Primarily, my jump-rope program is a general training exercise. It is not an exercise for building bigger shoulders. It is an exercise for building a bigger heart. Remember, as I've said earlier, rope jumping increases cardiovascular fitness by gradually conditioning your heart to accept a sustained rate of 130 to 150 beats per minute without fatigue. The exercise increases the volume of oxygen containing blood in the exercising muscles. It increases your capacity to process oxygen. Eventually, you will be able to process at least *twice* the amount of air per minute as the unfit or untrained person. You will increase the capacity of your lungs to about 75 percent. (Nobody uses full lung capacity; most of us, in fact, use about 33 percent)

Your blood vessels will become larger and more pliable, which usually causes a decrease in blood pressure. You will experience vascularization . . . an actual increase in the number of blood vessels. New networks of vessels develop to saturate muscle tissue with oxygen and remove waste more effectively.

Metabolism will become easier, particularly in breaking down fats, such as cholesterol. And jumping will help keep your arteries free of excess cholesterol. Muscle tissue becomes longer and leaner and closer to the oxygen supply in the blood vessels. The heavily involved muscles of the legs, arms, and shoulders will become stronger. The primary objective of all exercise programs is the conditioning of the heart to sustain at a higher rate without fatigue. Everything else is a bonus. You will cut your heart rate. And cutting that rate even by 10 to 15 beats per minute means you will be saving 15 to 20 thousand beats a day!

You will improve your digestion as the muscles of the digestive tract are conditioned.

You will lose weight, because you will change fat muscle into lean muscle. You will have better bust support, because jumping rope builds up your pectoral muscles, which support the breasts.

You will have more energy, less tension, and rest better, because you will be more able to meet energy demands . . . stress.

It makes you fit.

Someday soon, you will be able to develop a whole dazzling routine of several different jumps and twirls. A complete dance program is waiting for you later in this book. But I want you to get your heart ready first. Do not begin the advanced jumps and dance program until you have completed at least six weeks of my basic program.

As you embark on my jump-rope program, here are some things to remember:

1. Relax while you're jumping. Land gently. Jump lightly, lifting off from the toes and landing on the balls of your feet.

2. Use a long rope that reaches from armpit to armpit when you stand on the center of the rope.

3. Don't be upset by a tangled rope.

4. Jump to music if you can.

5. Master one step at a time until it's automatic.

6. Jump low. Not more than one inch off the floor.

7. Watch your pulse rate and make sure it stays within the recommended exercising rate for your age.

8. Practice a new step without the rope first. Then practice twirling the rope while jumping alongside.

9. Keep your head up and eyes straight ahead.

10. Keep both elbows and hands fairly close to the body.

11. Bend at the ankles, knees, and hips.

12. Let your hands, wrists, and lower arms do the turning.

13. Stay at your natural and prescribed skipping speed. Speed up later when you are ready.

14. Don't overdo it.

Here are some things you should *not* do:

1. Jump barefoot or in stocking feet.

2. Wear shoes with heels.

3. Use a rope that is too short or too long.

4. Jump too high.

5. Land flat-footed.

6. Look down while jumping.

7. Make too big a circle with your hands.

8. Hold the elbows too far from the hips.

9. Jump too fast while learning a new step.

10. Learn too many steps in too short a time.

11. Get mad at the rope because it tangles.

12. Get discouraged.

13. Suffer!

The Greg Campbell Life Chart
for Women
Suggested Programs

Week	Jumps per Minute	Times per Day	Days per Week	Under 30	31–39	40–49	50–59
1	60–70	3–4	5	1 min	1 min	1 min	1 min
2	60–70	2–3	5	2 min	2 min	1 min	1 min
3	60–70	2	5	4 min	3 min	2 min	1 min
4	70–80	2	5	5 min	4 min	4 min	3 min
5	70–80	2	5	6 min	5 min	4 min	4 min
6	70–80	1	5	8 min	8 min	6 min	6 min
7	80–90	1	5	10 min	8 min	6 min	6 min
8	80–90	1	5	11 min	9 min	7 min	7 min
9	80–90	1	5	12 min	10 min	9 min	8 min
10	90–100	1	5	13 min	11 min	10 min	9 min
11	90–100	1	5	13 min	11 min	10 min	9 min
12	100–120	1	5	14 min	12 min	11 min	10 min

The Greg Campbell Life Chart for Men
Suggested Programs

Week	Jumps per Minute	Times per Day	Days per Week	Under 30	31–39	40–49	50–59
1	60–70	3–4	5	1 min	1 min	1 min	1 min
2	60–70	2–3	5	2 min	2 min	1 min	1 min
3	70–80	2	5	4 min	3 min	3 min	2 min
4	70–80	2	5	6 min	4 min	4 min	3 min
5	80–90	1	5	8 min	5 min	4 min	4 min
6	80–90	1	5	11 min	7 min	6 min	5 min
7	80–90	1	5	12 min	9 min	7 min	6 min
8	90–100	1	5	13 min	10 min	7 min	6 min
9	90–100	1	5	13 min	11 min	9 min	7 min
10	90–100	1	5	13 min	11 min	10 min	9 min
11	90–100	1	5	13 min	11 min	10 min	9 min
12	100–120	1	5	14 min	12 min	11 min	10 min

XIV.
Jumping For Sports

Jumping rope is a natural, total body movement. Your legs, feet, arms, wrists, shoulders, back, and brain are involved in a coordinated, concentrated effort with each spin of the rope. Jumping helps your performance in sports. The general strength and endurance you gain will help you in any sport or other oxygen-consuming exercise. You'll suffer less from fatigue. You'll last longer in the game. You will be a stronger competitor.

Boxers have been jumping rope since there have been boxers, I think. Baseball players and football teams are working out on the rope now. So are professional basketball players. Each of these sports requires a high degree of hand-mind-feet coordination, as well as short high-oxygen consumption.

Jumping rope, in other words, is not only a great fitness exercise in itself, but an excellent warm-up and training exercise for improving your performance in sports.

Jumping rope involves *interval training*, that kind of exercise which requires short bursts of energy alternated with rest periods.

Such exercise is proven to be one of the best methods of strengthening the heart. With a stronger heart, legs, arms and wrists, flexible bones and joints, supple, heated muscles, developed hand-feet coordination, you are going to surprise some people on the golf course, tennis-handball-racketball court, swimming pool, softball diamond, ski-run, or whatever sport you are into. Most of all, you are going to surprise yourself.

FOR GENERAL SPORTS TRAINING

All sports require endurance, concentration, coordination, strength, mobility, and agility to some degree. Your oxygen-consumption ability plays an important part in your performance in any sport. Jumping rope will aid you.

Secondly, rope jumping strengthens certain parts of the body. Parts that play major roles in certain sports. These parts, like legs, arms and wrists, do not necessarily get bigger but stronger.

84

Thirdly, nothing is more essential than warming up to sports activity. Warming up does not mean donning a track suit and working up a sweat. (Indeed, that means you may have gone too far and expended energy to a point which saps the strength you want for your sport.)

In warming up for any sport, all you need is to gently raise your pulse rate to between 110 and 120 beats a minute for a few minutes.

Your body, particularly your muscles, work better, easier, and with less strain when they are heated. When you begin physical activity, every gram of glucose fuel demanded by the muscles releases about four calories of energy. Now, almost 75 percent of these calories are used to generate heat, and the remaining calories are utilized to actually work the muscle. For each Celsius degree of temperature rise in the muscle, the metabolic rate of the muscle cells (the speed with which energy can be produced) increases by 14 percent. Warmer muscles mean faster available energy.

Also, physical activity signals a certain fluid lying between cartilage plates to get thicker. This fluid, as it thickens, serves as a body lubricant to cushion the new strain on your joints.

Warm-up exercises prepare your body for the strain of sport.

RACKET GAMES AND ROPE SKIPPING

The most effective preparatory exercises for different sports are those which duplicate the effort and movement involved in the sport. Racket games require strength in the racket hand, arm and wrist, with support of the shoulder and flexibility in the trunk, muscular strength in the legs, and cardiovascular efficiency to withstand sudden intense sports across the court.

Refer to my chart for your particular jumping speed according to your age, sex, and progress. Prior to the racket game, jump for one minute using the *One-Two Jump.*(See Chapter XIII for instructions on these jumps.) Rest for 10 seconds, and jump for another 60 seconds, using the *Jogging Jump.* Rest for 20 seconds, and use the *Jogging Jump* or the *One-Two Jump* and initiate the *Double-Jump* (in which the rope passes under the feet twice while you jump once) and *cross over* two or three times during the 60 seconds. This will limber up your arms, wrists, and hands.

GOLF AND ROPE SKIPPING

Here's another sport that, though much less strenuous, demands strong wrists.

Refer to my life chart for your particular jumping speed if you are jumping to gradually improve your performance on the links. If you are warming up for a game, jump at 80 to 90 turns per minute.

In either case, use the alternate *Double-Jump* and concentrate on wrist and hand action.

Attempt as many *Cross-Overs* as you can. Eventually, you should be able to *Cross-Over* every two jumps.

If warming up before a game, jump at the above pace, applying several *Cross-Overs* for three to five minutes.

SKIING AND ROPE SKIPPING

Refer to my life chart for your particular speed and endurance program. Utilize the *Two-Footed Jump* and apply *Double-Jumps* as many times as possible. Try to jump higher each time you make a Double-Jump. Next, slow your turns to about 80 per minute and begin concentrating on lowering your body into a crouching position as you jump. DO NOT ATTEMPT THIS UNTIL YOU ARE FOUR WEEKS INTO MY PROGRAM.

Bring your body as low as you can, gradually, while still jumping. This is a taxing exercise. But so is skiing. Skiing sets the feet, legs, and knees at angles unlike those demanded by any other sport. Your bones and muscles at these points must be strong, supple, and toned. While you are jumping in a crouched position, you are simulating a downhill run. While you are leaping on the double-jump, you are simulating skiing over sudden rises and dips.

When warming up for actual skiing, jump at a slower pace, concentrating on the jumping and crouching. Warm up for five minutes.

DANCING AND ROPE SKIPPING

After you have mastered my basic steps, go directly to the dance steps in the intermediate stage. Concentrate on the kick and heel-and-toe steps. If you want to be a better dancer socially or professionally, these steps will keep your legs and feet coordinated, quick, and agile.

JOGGING AND ROPE SKIPPING.

Jumping rope offers one of the most concentrated leg exercises known. As a result, joggers who also jump improve strength and endurance.

After mastering my basic steps, concentrate on jumping to the *Jogging*

Jump and the *One-Two-Jump.* Warm up to jogging by jumping rope to the jogging step for three to five minutes prior to running out the door.

COMPETITION AND JUMPING ROPE

Rather than enter competition cold, you should warm up to it. Competition means stress. Mental stress can make as many demands on the body as physical stress. If you are not ready, you face the possibility of overreacting, overtensing and straining, trying too hard. Stress for the unfit can be devastating. So whether you plan to spend more time at a particular sport or want a good warm-up prior to it, jump. Rope skipping reduces stress. Jump rope first. Later, you can play tennis.

The best way to warm up for a sport is to practice non-competitively for five minutes. This will get your physical and mental system ready to win. After exerting sports exercises, warm down slowly. When you are active, all the blood vessels of the body open to help circulation to the muscles, which squeeze blood to the heart. If you stop suddenly after a hard session of racketball and just stand still with vessels still dilated, the heart has trouble keeping up the supply to some areas. Gravity pulls the blood away from your brain and could cause dizziness and swollen ankles. To avoid this, after the big game, bounce up and down, walk around, and keep moving for a while.

XV.
Dance, Dance, Dance

There are rope steps and there are rope steps. And there are more rope steps.

There are steps where the rope is turned sidesaddle with one hand over the head, the other near the knees. Some people can let the rope wrap around them and unwrap again into a loop without missing a hop. There are rope tricksters who use a very long rope and spin it, using only the wrists, with arms outstretched. There is no end to what you can do with a jump rope and what a jump rope can do with you.

You may already be a "disco dancer." I'm going to teach you to be a "disco jumper."

STEP VARIATIONS

Before trying the Greg Campbell Dance Program, accomplish the following advanced jumps: the Double-Triple Twirl, the Twirls, the Cross-Over, the Twirly-Bird and the Flip. These movements are impressive and, once accomplished, fun and exciting to execute. Apply these jumps while doing your basic steps and finish with the Flip. Accomplish these jumps and you will become a dancer. Polish my dance routine and you will belong in show business.

The Double-Triple Twirl

Jump high enough to allow the rope to revolve two or three
times over your head and beneath your feet before you land.
Remember to speed the rope up.

The Twirls

As the rope passes over your head, bring both hands together, closing the loop. Then twirl the rope in front of your body from side to side as you continue to jump. Continue twirling the rope from side to side like a windmill.

The Cross-Over

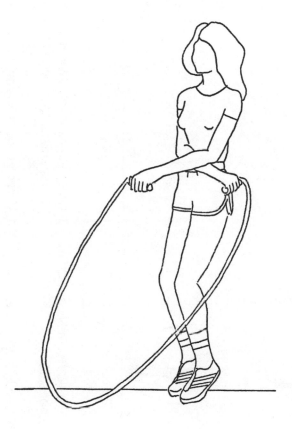

A very impressive stunt. While you are jumping, simply cross
your arms in front of your body. As the rope descends, jump
through the loop. As you continue, uncross your arms after the
rope passes beneath your feet. Make sure you cross your
arms at the elbows. Crossing at the wrists will cause a loop too
small to jump through.

The Twirly-Bird

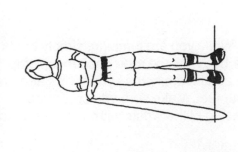

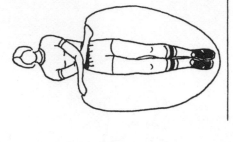

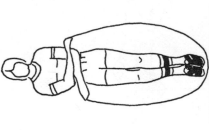

This stunt is the same as the cross-over, only you add a second cross-over from the other side.

1. Using both hands, twirl the rope in front of your body from side to side.

2. Now cross your right arm over your left, as you did in the Cross-Over. Cross over and jump through the loop once.

3. Cross your left arm over your right. Cross over and jump through the loop again.

4. Uncross your arms after the rope passes beneath your feet and continue to jump.

The Flip

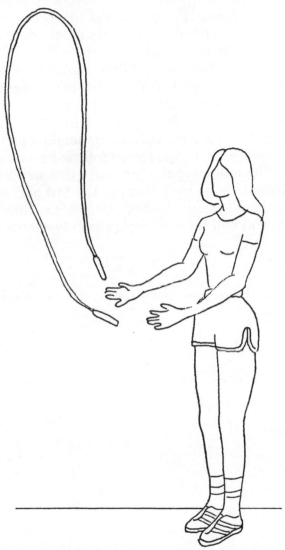

As the loop of the rope rises, toss the rope upward as you let go of the handles, causing the rope to revolve once in mid-air. Watch the handles as they finish the turn and grab them as the rope descends.

WAIT FOR APPLAUSE.

THE GREG CAMPBELL DANCE PROGRAM

I suppose the possibility of rope skipping becoming an Olympic event is slim. But imagine, if you will, a whole routine of jumping steps choreographed into a dance. I've performed this routine on television programs and discos in major cities. It looks much more difficult than it really is. It's dazzling to watch and fun to do.

What's dancing without music? Start looking for your favorite dancing numbers. If you're a basketball player, for example, jumping rope to improve your agility under the boards, put on "Sweet Georgia Brown." It works for the Harlem Globetrotters. I like the sound of "Saturday Night Fever" or "Native New Yorker," depending on my mood. Today's disco sound is perfect in tempo for the following dance steps.

In learning the following routine, learn one step variation at a time. When you learn two, go back through the first and second. When you learn three, go back through the first, second, and third.

Eventually, you will have all eighteen movements into one continuous routine.

Two-Footed Jump

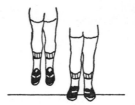

Tap the floor in front of you with your right heel while you jump on your left foot.

Return and continue on.

Tap the floor in front of you with your left heel while you jump on your right foot.

Return and continue on.

Two-Footed Jump

Tap the floor in back of you with your right toe.

Return and continue on.

Tap the floor in back of you with your left toe.

Return and continue on.

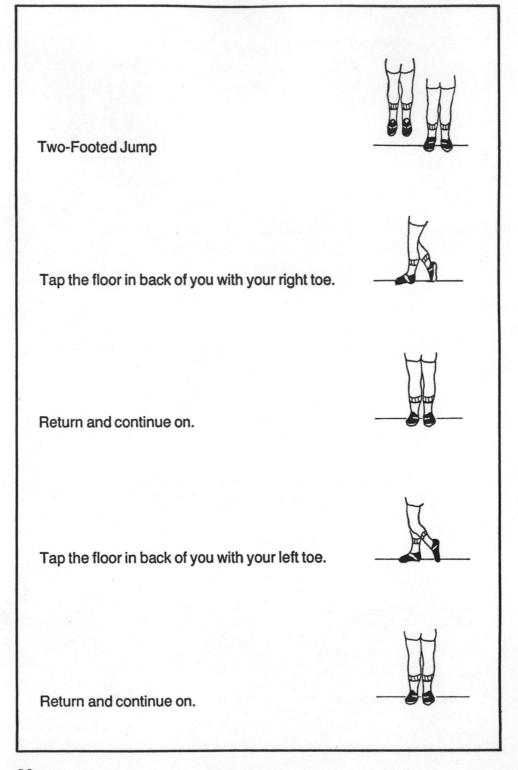

Two-Footed Jump

Tap your right heel in front of you while you do a left-foot jump.

Tap your right toe in back of you while you do a left-foot jump.

Change to your left foot.

Tap your left heel in front of you while you do a right-foot jump.

Tap your left toe in back of you while you do a right-foot jump.

Return and continue on.

Two-Footed Jump

Tap your right heel in front of you while you do a left-foot jump.

Cross your right foot to the left in front of your jumping foot and tap the floor with your right toe.

Tap your right heel in front of you while you do a left-foot jump.

Return and continue on, using the same procedure with your left foot.

Two-Footed Jump

Tap your right toe in back of you while you do a left-foot jump.

Cross your right foot behind you and to the left of your jumping foot and tap the floor with your right toe.

Tap your right toe in back of you while you do a left-foot jump.

Return and continue on using the same procedure with your left foot.

Two-Footed Jump

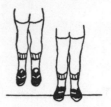

Tap your right heel in front of you while you do a left-foot jump.

Cross your right foot to the left in front of your jumping foot and tap the floor with your right toe.

Tap your right heel in front of you while you do a left-foot jump.

Tap your right toe in back of you while you do a left-foot jump.

Return and continue on.

Two-Footed Jump

Tap your right heel in front of you while you do a left-foot jump.

Touch your left knee with your right heel while you do a left-foot jump.

Tap your right heel in front of you while you do a left-foot jump.

Tap your right toe in back of you while you do a left-foot jump.

Return and continue on.

Two-Footed Jump

While doing a left-foot jump, spread your right leg sideward and tap the floor with your right foot.

Return and continue on, using the same procedure with your left leg.

Two-Footed Jump

Spread your legs sideward, jumping on the balls of your feet. (Remember jumping jacks in school?)

Return and continue on.

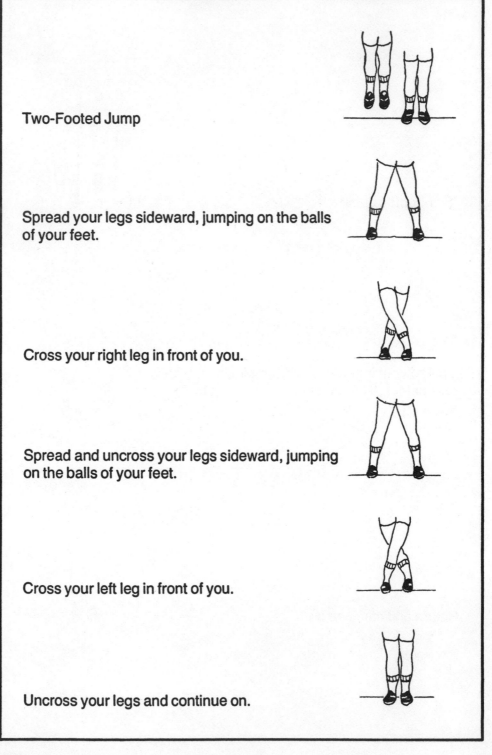

Two-Footed Jump

Spread your legs sideward, jumping on the balls of your feet.

Cross your right leg in front of you.

Spread and uncross your legs sideward, jumping on the balls of your feet.

Cross your left leg in front of you.

Uncross your legs and continue on.

Two-Footed Jump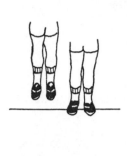

Cross your right leg in front of you.

Uncross and then recross your left leg in front of you.

Return and continue on.

Two-Footed Jump

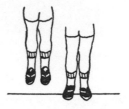

Spread your legs sideward, jumping on the balls of your feet.

Jump up and click your heels together and then land, jumping on the balls of your feet.

Return and do it again. It's fun. Then continue on for more fun.

Two-Footed Jump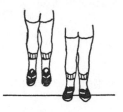

Jump slightly to your right, using your right foot, and fling your left foot backward at the same time.

Jump slightly to your left, using your left foot, and fling your right foot backward at the same time.

Return and continue on.

Two-Footed Jump

Jump forward on your right foot and then extend your left leg backward, forcing yourself to bend a little at your waist.

Kick your right foot forward and lean backward and land on your left foot.

Jump forward on your right foot and then extend your left leg backward, forcing yourself to bend a little at your waist.

Return and continue on.

Two-Footed Jump

Keep your right leg straight and then fling it out to your right while you do a left-foot jump.

Keep your left leg straight and then fling it out to your left while you do a right-foot jump.

Return and continue on.

Two-Footed Jump

Jump up and keep your knees together, flinging
your right leg forward and your left leg backward.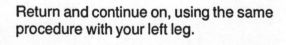

Return and continue on, using the same
procedure with your left leg.

Two-Footed Jump

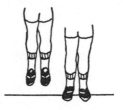

Jump on your left foot and then twist your right toe outward and tap your right toe on the floor.

Jump on your left foot and then twist your right toe inward and tap your right toe on the floor.

Return and continue on.

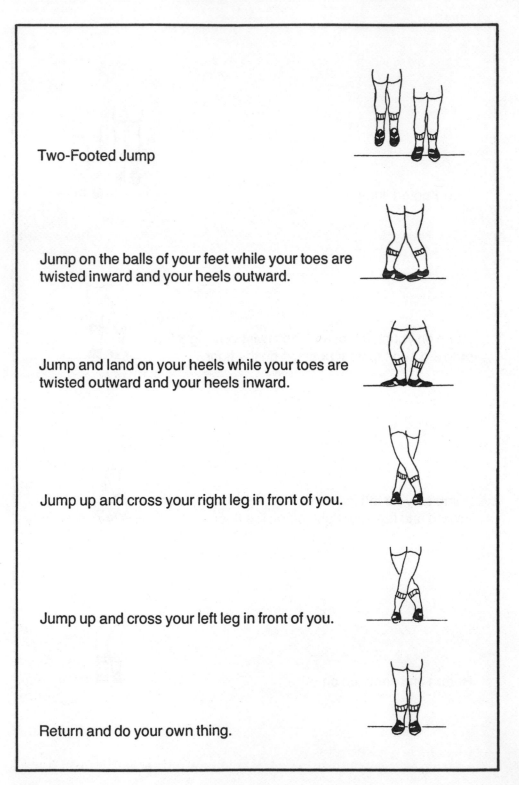

Two-Footed Jump

Jump on the balls of your feet while your toes are twisted inward and your heels outward.

Jump and land on your heels while your toes are twisted outward and your heels inward.

Jump up and cross your right leg in front of you.

Jump up and cross your left leg in front of you.

Return and do your own thing.

XVI.
How to Fight Boredom

Frustration or boredom is always lurking around the corner whenever we work. And jumping rope is work. Despite the flashy, dazzling jumps I've taught you and the impressive dance routine you've learned, all exercise has some degree of tedium in it.

Here are some ideas to help you overcome boredom:

1. TRY JUMPING WHILE YOU DO SOMETHING ELSE

While you are jumping to music, try singing the words. See how long it takes you in your program to sing while jumping without sounding out of breath. The trick is to find a short song. You should have no problem with a two-and-a-half-minute song if you are jumping at the five-minute level. Later on, when you develop your own routine, you can sing *and* dance to your music.

Five-minute radio newscasts can help you set your routine. Suppose you've selected a broadcast like: "Good Morning. It's 7:25 A.M. and time for the latest news from WHAP." There you are. Five minutes of input and output at the same time. Or use television the same way. If you are jumping at the three-minute rate, wait until after the headlines and stop when you hear: "We'll have the weather after this message . . ."

2. SHARE YOUR ROPE

Two can jump as quickly (not as easily) as one. Once you get the rope turning, have someone jump the loop with you. The Two-Footed Jump works best. Your partner must face you and stand close to you. If you are really looking for excitement, see if the two of you can complete the double-triple twirl together, for example. You may have to use a longer rope for this trick.

Imagine several of you side-by-side, working the Greg Campbell Dance Program in coordination.

Speaking of togetherness, encourage your family to join you in jumping. Mom and Dad can be the "enders" (people who twirl the ends of a rope). The children can jump in and out, as you used to do.

I know one jump-rope record I haven't seen. What's the earliest age a child has learned to jump rope? Try teaching your pre-schooler how to jump. It may work. Teach your husband or wife how to jump, too.

3. TALK IT UP

Sometimes you just need some spiritual encouragement about your exercise. Talk it up. Talk about fitness. The facts and figures about fitness in this workbook are enough to get you started. They represent some of the latest findings on fitness and cardiovascular efficiency. Become an expert.

4. MAKE A GAME OUT OF IT

As a child, you had your favorite rhymes and chants to jump by. Now, you're jumping for a different reason. How about making up some new words to old songs?

5. GO SOMEWHERE

It's a beautiful day and you'd like to go somewhere while you are exercising. If you would like to sacrifice convenience for adventure and skip and run at the same time, give it a try but be careful. Remember, a tangle while jumping in place is mild compared to the pitfalls you face when you are moving forward.

You'll have to go at a pretty good clip to run and skip at 80 turns a minute. Be aware, too, that you probably won't be high-stepping, so watch out for your heels as they come up in back of you. If you run and skip, don't just look straight ahead. Look where you are going. Take the kids along with you.

6. DON'T FORCE YOURSELF

There are humps to get over in rope jumping. Hard spots. Transitions from one level of fitness to another. Two plateaus, the five-minute and ten-minute duration levels, are very important. Don't force yourself into them. Remember the myth we unloaded at the beginning of this book? *You don't have to struggle to get one more than yesterday.* Let it happen naturally. If you force yourself, you will be slipping back into the old exercise school for another bleak semester. And there is no reason to face that kind of discouragement. If you are not able to keep pace with the progression level, hold back a few days or a week. Do not overextend yourself. Do not dwell on reaching the five- or ten-minute plateau. Concentrate on what you are doing at the moment and make it reasonable. Let that additional minute or increase in rope speed happen naturally and become a pleasant surprise. I want you to become out of breath. But nobody's asking you to run the four-minute mile. I just want you to be able to get the groceries out of the car and into the house easily, effortlessly.

7. Slow Down

Check your speed. Many times jumpers get fatigued before their required time expires because they are jumping too fast. Don't speed up your jumps to get the required number over with. The program is carefully designed as a combination of increasing levels of duration and difficulty.

XVII.
The Greg Campbell Pep Talk

It pleases me to know that the jump rope is more popular today than it ever was in the past. But there is a danger in fads.

Fads come and go. Somebody is going to thumb through this book, try a few steps for a while, and say: "Well, that was nice, but I'm not going to spend the rest of my life learning all those steps. What else is new?"

It's natural, particularly with a workbook, to just open it to the program, pick up a rope, and give it a whirl. And if you are an accomplished jumper, it could work for you. Maybe you just wanted to learn some new steps, so you turn directly to the section on intermediate and advanced jumping.

If you are like most people in terms of fitness and ability, however, that won't help you. My curiosity is frustrating sometimes. That's why I'm not very good at reading mystery stories. I think too much about a premature look at the last page to see "who done it." You picked up a book on an exciting, new, and simple exercise program and you find thirteen chapters on why instead of how. To tell you the truth, mental attitude is a worn-out, overused phrase that still maintains its validity. I do want you to know why you are jumping. What it means to your mind, spirit, and body. Fitness has been a scary word to us, a guilt-making word. Something we knew we all needed, but didn't have the time or energy to acquire. It took me thirteen chapters to demonstrate to you that fitness need not be frightening and that, with the right thinking, you can become fit and change your life so easily it really is a laugh.

If you decide to look to the last chapter to see "who done it," I prefer you look at this chapter and discover that if you sustain this program, you will find out "who done it." *You* did!

Suppose, after the initial novelty, you put the book away and say: "Well, I'll get back to it one of these days." Excuse me but I think the buck ought to stop right here. I think it is time you stopped putting your life off until tomorrow. Exercise, even the perfect exercise, is work. There are no magic pills that will make you fit. Nothing or no one can do it but you. This time, then, you haven't found a fad, an "in" thing. You have found the shortest, simplest route to physical, mental, and emotional fitness.

You have found a way to change your life. You can slow the aging process, improve your digestion, stay shapely, give your bust better support, sleep better, have more energy, relax your nerves, stabilize your emotions, improve your skin tone, perform better at work and at sports, enhance your sexuality, strengthen your heart and lungs and muscles and bones, and discover an inner peace you never believed possible.

Think about that each time you decide to hang it up, each time the rope tangles mercilessly around your feet, each time your heart pounds and you are out of breath, each time you see a jogger plodding along in a rainstorm, each time you notice how much your children have grown.

If you want to simplify things, think about another "scary" phrase: "Only the strong survive." And realize that you can be as strong as the next bruiser, as strong as the defensive end on the Dallas Cowboys. You may be able to lift as much weight, but strength is only one third of being strong. Flexibility and stamina are the other two thirds—flexibility or the joint mobility to move your body gracefully, effectively, with a minimum expenditure of energy, whether it's to blitz the quarterback or mow the lawn. Stamina, endurance, depends on the capacity of your heart and circulation to supply blood and oxygen to the various parts of your body in times of energy crisis. Your energy potential can become as great as the Olympian, the long-distance runner, the athlete, someone twenty or thirty years younger than you.

You can do all this by moving. Move at a level beyond and above your normal day of movements. Don't quit jumping or moving ever. Give yourself some time. There is a lot at stake. Eventually, all you will need is ten minutes of a special exercise five days a week.

Form a habit. When you determine what time of day it is best for you to exercise, stick to it. Keep that time as special and sacred.

Suppose you decide to play hooky one or two days during your exercise program. How do you make it up? You don't. Just resume at the pace you left off and add two days. Don't play catch up. Just because you missed two days worth four minutes of jumping, jumping six minutes on the third day is not the most efficient way of progressing.

Is one jump better than none at all? Physiologists declare that increased cardiovascular efficiency can only be achieved when a high-energy exercise is applied for a minimum length of time and difficulty at regular intervals and that you must have physical activity that transcends energy you expend during your normal day.

So suppose you mess up one day and do only fifty jumps, or ten, or one, and you have to stop because the lights went out or something. Was what you did do a waste? No. True, you did little to increase your cardiovascular system's capacity. But anytime you move above and beyond what you normally do, you are getting exercise. You are increasing, even though on a much smaller level, your energy potential. Because you at least jumped, you helped your attitude too. You tried.

To develop endurance, you must exercise for at least two or three minutes at a time and it must be sufficiently vigorous to bring the heart rate up to the 70 percent of maximum level. It must cause you to be out of breath.

Remember, though, exercise, like sleep, cannot be caught up on.

Keep your faith in this program. It works.

Enjoy jumping because it's effective and fun and exciting and challenging.

Give yourself rewards for the effort you have applied. If you are dieting, yes, splurge on yourself once in a while.

Go to a party, go dancing, do something for yourself for working to become a better you.

If you stop, make it temporary. Explain to yourself what happened or why you stopped the program and offer forgiveness if you promise to start again.

Completing the entire program should create enough of a habit in you that you continue to jump. You can become fit in this time period. What then? The capacity to produce energy is like energy itself in the body. It just can't be saved up. Your body doesn't work like a flashlight battery. Face it. Creating an energy potential is a lifelong process. The fact is that fitness will definitely erode without maintenance.

A week of bed rest can extract 10 percent of your bone mass—even after three months of a cardiovascular exercise program. You've overcome the hardest part of an exercise program by completing my program: You've overcome inertia. You have started moving. So keep moving. Jump, hop, skip, run, and walk whenever you can. Bounce up and down at the checkout counter at the supermarket. Who cares?

Instead of waiting in the car for your spouse, get out and jump up and down while you wait. "One-Two," "One-Two." Play football with the kids. Dance more. Hop while you're waiting at the bus stop on a cold day.

KEEP MOVING

Remember not to lie down when you can sit up, don't sit when you can stand, don't just stand there when you can walk, don't walk when you can run and jump.

KEEP MOVING.   And good luck!

118

Appendix

A Summary of Fitness Facts

The Exercise Myth

Fitness does not have to be achieved at the cost of bodily discomfort.

Working up a sweat is not essential to fitness.

You do not need to wear a sweatsuit or a rubberized suit to stay warm while exercising.

You do not need to put on a sweater or something to keep warm after exercising.

You do not need a cold shower after exercise.

Consuming additional protein will not give you more energy.

Eating extra sugar does not give you the right extra energy.

You do not need to take salt tablets while exercising.

You do not need to abstain from drinking while exercising.

You do not need more sleep while in an exercise program.

You do not need to exercise an hour every day. Five to fifteen minutes are enough if you are in the right program.

You do not have to suffer to become fit.

The Heart of the Matter

The primary benefit of any correct exercise program is the improvement of your heart rate.

Today's medical authorities agree that cardiovascular fitness is the most valid indicator of a person's relative physical fitness.

A strong heart is a slow heart.

Unless your cardiovascular system can deliver enough oxygen for proper fuel conversion, your system becomes atrophic.

Exercise the most important muscle in your body by exercising the muscular system.

A strong heart helps you expand the vital capacity of the lungs, which means taking in more air.

Cardiovascular fitness must be achieved gradually by means of a week-by-week program of increasing difficulty.

THE PERFECT EXERCISE

While isometric exercises do increase strength and muscle tone rapidly, they will not improve the heart and blood system and lungs, nor will they increase oxygen intake.

Jumping rope is the best all-around exercise you can find.

It's efficient and effective: There is nothing you can spend less time on that will give you more results.

It's inexpensive: all you need is a rope.

It's convenient. You can jump in an area as small as a walk-in closet.

It's not boring: There is always something new to do. New steps, more speed. Longer duration.

It's practical: It's small enough to fit in a purse or a coat pocket, needs a minimum of repair, and is practically noiseless.

Its simple: Hopping is a simple, natural function you've done all your life.

It's fun: Jumping rope has variety and looks impressive.

WHAT RESEARCH TELLS US

In summary, the research data indicate that rope skipping is a worthwhile activity for the development of muscular strength and endurance, cardiovascular fitness, balance, agility, and coordination.

JUMPING FOR HEALTH

Fitness is the capacity of your body to perform work.

The American man ranks only seventeenth, the American woman ranks tenth, in longevity among the major nations of the world.

More than half the deaths in the United States are attributed to cardiovascular disease.

These factors affect your health: heredity, smoking, drinking, obesity, poor diet, and lack of exercise. We don't rust out, we wear out.

It was once believed that physical activity added to the wear and tear on the body tissues and advanced the aging process. We know now that the opposite is true.

The President's Council on Physical Fitness states: ". . . regular exercise can help prevent degenerative disease and slow down the physical deterioration that accompanies aging."

A well-trained 65-year-old may be superior in physical capacity to an untrained 35-year-old.

JUMPING FOR SPORTS

Jumping improves your ability at sports and serves as an efficient warm-up before the contest. See jump-rope programs designed specifically to develop you in tennis, badminton, racketball and handball, golf, skiing, jogging, and dancing.

JUMPING FOR SEX

If you feel flabby, out-of-shape, and unappealing, you'll send that message to your partner and there will be no sensuality. Tension and stress from life's frustrations can deter your sexual interest and ability. Exercise is a natural way to relieve tension.

THE STRESS FACTOR

Social stress acts as a kind of population control. It is also a maimer and a killer. Medical science measures fitness in terms of one's ability to tolerate stress. Continuous high-level stress has physical effects that can be fatal.

Half the beds in American hospitals are occupied by mental patients.

Emotional stress can harm the unfit.

The stress of illness can make an unfit patient sicker.

Physical fatigue combined with sleeplessness is often an indicator of lack of exercise.

Physical, emotional, psychological, and mental fatigues are all states in which you owe your body more oxygen than you are giving it.

Hopping or jumping is a natural way of moving, especially under stress conditions.

LIGHTEN THE LOAD

You do not necessarily have to be fat to be flabby. It takes a combination of the right diet and the right exercise to be at your proper weight and proper proportions. The pinch test involves gathering an inch of pinch at your waist or underarms. An inch of pinch reflects forty pounds of fat. Any more and you are overweight.

You can actually lose weight and gain fat if muscles atrophy. Don't be fooled by the scale.

Jumping rope may not change your basic shape, but it will change your appearance.

On being overweight: 25 percent of Americans are at least fifteen pounds overweight.

A man 20 percent overweight increases his chance for an early death by 20 percent. Fat people commit suicide more often, have more accidents, more heart attacks, more bladder disease, more arthritis, and more backaches.

If you weigh ten to twenty pounds over your ideal body weight, you are overweight.

Losing weight in a hurry can be harmful by causing a loss in body tissue.

The only way to lose fat permanently is slowly, not more than a pound a week. You want to burn the right amount of fat while maintaining your normal metabolic rate.

One pound of flesh is equivalent to 3,500 calories. To lose a pound, you must burn off 3,500 more calories than you eat.

The right diet, combined with the right exercise, is the painless way to lose fat, because you maintain your body's healthy balance, lose weight permanently, tone and trim your body, and gain strength and energy all at the same time.

WHO CAN JUMP

Anyone who is physically able and has been given clearance by his or her physician may jump rope.

It increases fitness in people from 7 to 70. Regardless of your current activity, to develop fitness, you must exercise and expend energy over and above the normal demands of your day.

Whether you are a "night" person or a "morning" person, due to your biological rhythm, jump during the time of day that's best for you.

Jump before eating if you are dieting.

Jump when you feel any stress.

ON THE ROPES

You may fashion your own rope out of a simple sash cord, or purchase a commercial rope that ranges in cost from three to ten dollars. Remember, you can try tennis with a Ping-Pong paddle, too, so find a rope that best suits your needs and earnestness about becoming fit.

Proper length of the rope is important. Measure by standing in the middle of the rope with one foot. The handles or ends should reach under your armpits.

Wear a supportive bra or supportive underwear. Do not wear tight-fitting clothing or non-porous attire such as windbreakers or rubberized sweatsuits.

Wear shoes. Do not jump barefoot or in stocking feet.

FIRING UP

It is a necessity that you recieve a medical assessment of your present state of fitness, especially if you are overweight or over 30.

Take the simple fitness tests as we have outlined. If you fail one of them, spend a week at our preparatory exercises before your first week of jumping rope.

It is important that you warm up with exercises prior to any time you take part in a rigorous exercise such as jumping rope or a sport activity. This heats the muscles and prepares them for the shock.

It is equally important that you cool down by walking around immediately after a cardiovascular activity to prevent the blood from pooling in the lower legs and creating dizziness and swelling.

Check your pulse regularly.

Your second week of regular activity consists of learning the three basic jumps without the rope and learning to turn the rope without jumping over it.

If you are fifteen pounds overweight or in the advanced-age category, follow the special programs designed for you. Otherwise, if you have medical clearance, follow the general program according to your age, whether you are sedentary or feel physically fit.

Prior to and during the program, follow the heart rate guide as a measure of your not exceeding 70 percent of your maximum average heart rate for your age.

Our goal is to gradually increase your exercising heart rate to between 130 and 150 beats per minute while lowering your resting heart rate.

Additional benefits of a rope-jumping program are:

To increase your capacity to produce oxygen to a point where you will be able to process at least twice the amount of air per minute as the unfit or untrained person.

To increase your vital capacity of about 75 percent of total lung capacity.

To make your vessels larger and more piable, which usually causes a decrease in blood pressure.

To create vascularization: the growth of new networks of vessels.

To make metabolism more efficient in breaking down fat.

To strengthen the muscles of your legs, arms, shoulders, and stomach.

To improve your digestion by toning the muscles of your digestive tract.

To reduce weight by changing fat tissue into protein tissue.

To create better bust support by strengthening pectoral muscles.

To create more energy to cope with stress and fatigue.

DANCE, DANCE, DANCE

Make up your own rhymes out of the old ones you knew as a child.

Jump to music.

Don't force yourself.

Don't jump faster than your level.

Jump while listening to the radio or watching television.

Jump with a partner.

Jump with your family.

Try jumping while running, but be careful.

One jump is better than none.

Talk about fitness.

CALORIE EXPENDITURE IN VARIOUS SPORTS AND EXERCISE ACTIVITIES (BY PERSON OF 150 POUNDS)

ACTIVITY	APPROXIMATE CALORIE EXPENDITURE PER HOUR
Bicycling (5½ mph)	210
Walking (2½ mph)	210
Canoeing (2½ mph)	230
Golf	250
Bowling	270
Swimming (¼ mph)	300
Badminton	350
Volleyball	350
Table Tennis	360
Ice Skating (10 mph)	400
Tennis	420
Water-Skiing	480
Skiing (10 mph)	600
Squash and Handball	600
Running (5.7 mph)	720
Skipping Rope (120–140 turns per min.)	760
Running (9.0 mph)	*900*

Bibliography

BOOKS

Ald, Roy, *Jogging, Aerobics and Diet.* New York, 1968.
Cooper, Kenneth, *Aerobics.* New York, 1968.
Cooper, Mildred, *Aerobics for Women.* New York, 1972.
Gore, Irene, *Add Years to Your Life and Life to Your Years.* New York, 1973.
Higdon, Hal, *Fitness After Forty.* New York, 1977.
Mitchell, Curtis, *The Perfect Exercise.*
Morehouse, Laurence, *Total Fitness.* New York, 1975.
Rodhal, Dr. Kaare, *Be Fit For Life.* New York, 1966.
Rodale, Robert, *The Best Health Ideas I Know.* New York, 1974.
     Rand McNally Company, *Feel Younger, Live Longer.* New York, 1976.
Rosenberger, Magda, *Sixty Plus and Fit Again.* Philadelphia, 1977.
Skolnick, Peter L., *Jump Rope!* New York, 1974.

PERIODICALS

Physical Fitness Research Digest, October, 1977.

PUBLICATIONS AND ARTICLES

Baker, John A. "Comparison of Rope Skipping and Jogging As Methods of Improving Cardiovascular Efficiency of College Men," *Research Quarterly*, May, 1968.
Ball, Florence J. "A Comparison of Four Methods of Developing Physical Fitness in Junior High School Girls," unpublished master's thesis, Arkansas State College, 1966.
Cascino, Joseph A. "The Effects of a Program of Progressive Rope Skipping on the Cardiovascular Fitness of Adult Men," unpublished master's thesis, Temple University, 1964.

Clarke, H. Harrison, *Muscular Strength and Endurance in Man,* Prentice Hall, Inc., 1966. Chapter 5.

Curtis, Delores May. "Rope Skipping and the Endurance, Leg Power, Agility, and Coordination of Children," unpublished doctoral dissertation, the University of Illinois, 1963.

Donaghe, Sheila J. "The Effect of a Ten-Minute Period of Progressive Rope Jumping Exercise on Certain Elements of Physical Fitness and on Badminton Achievement of College Women," unpublished master's thesis, University of Washington, 1963.

Durrant, Arlene, "The Effects of Jogging, Rope Jumping and Aerobic Dance on Body Composition and Maximum Oxygen Uptake of College Females," doctoral dissertation, Brigham Young University, 1975.

Fahey, Helen. "Everyone Jumps Rope," *Journal of Health and Physical Education,* September, 1940.

Franklin, Barbara J. "The Effect of a Progressive Period of Rope Skipping in Beginning Fencing Classes on Wrist Flexibility and Strength and on the Execution of Fencing Parries by College Women," unpublished master's thesis, University of Washington, 1966.

Garrett, Leon, Mohammed Sabie, and Roy Pangle. "Four Approaches to Increasing Cardiovascular Fitness During Volleyball Instruction," *Research Quarterly,* December, 1965.

Hathaway, Gordon J. "Modern Rope Skipping," *Journal of Health, Physical Education and Recreation,* May, 1955.

Jones, D. Marritt, Chadwick Squires and Kaare Rodahl, "Effect of Rope Skipping on Physical Work Capacity," *Research Quarterly,* May, 1962.

Kobayshi, Yoshio. "The Effect of Rope Jumping on Cardio-Respiratory Fitness of High School Students," unpublished master's thesis, Eastern Illinois University, 1969.

Lofgren, Audrey. "Effects of Progressive Rope Skipping Training Bouts on Recovery Pulse Rate and Strength of Foot Extension," unpublished master's thesis, South Dakota State University, 1966.

Melby, Rolf E. "Rope Jumping, " *Journal of Health and Physical Education,* February, 1936.

"National Adult Physical Fitness Survey," Newsletter, President's Council on Physical Fitness and Sports, Special Edition, May, 1973.

Powell, John T. "The Effects of a Program on Progressive Rope Skipping on Prepubescent Boys," graduate thesis, University of Illinois, 1957.

Prentup, Frank B. *Skipping The Rope for Fun and Fitness,* Boulder, Colorado, 1963.

Scholnick, Tony. "A Comparison of the Effects of Selected Exercises, Isometrics and Isotonics on the Explosive Power and Leg Strength, unpublished master's thesis, Springfield College, 1964.

Smith, Paul, *Rope Skipping: Rhythms, Routines, Rhymes,* Educational Activities, Inc., 1969.

Wattenbarger, Sondra, "The Effects of Pacing on Heart Rates During Rope Jumping," unpublished master's thesis, Oklahoma State University, 1969.

Wilber, Helen, "Plus Values for Rope Jumping," *Journal of Health, Physical Education and Recreation*, February, 1966.